THE
NEWCASTLE
MISCELLANY

THE
NEWCASTLE
MISCELLANY

BY MIKE BOLAM

VSP

Vision Sports Publishing
2 Coombe Gardens,
London SW20 0QU

www.visionsp.co.uk

Published by Vision Sports Publishing 2007

ISBN 10: 1-905326-18-1
ISBN 13: 978-1-905326-18-1

Printed and bound in the UK by
Cromwell Press Ltd, Trowbridge, Wiltshire

Typeset by Palimpsest Book Production Limited,
Grangemouth, Stirlingshire

A CIP catalogue record for this book is
available from the British Library

Mixed Sources
Product group from well-managed
forests and other controlled sources
www.fsc.org Cert no. TT-COC-2082
© 1996 Forest Stewardship Council

Vision Sports Publishing are
proud that this book is made
from paper certified by the
Forest Stewardship Council

Author's Acknowledgements

I would like to thank Paul Joannou and Alan Candlish for their encouragement and assistance in writing this book, as well as Jim Drewett and Clive Batty at Vision Sports Publishing for helping me produce it.

Credit is also due to my co-writer at NUFC.com, Niall Mackenzie and the readers of that website for their input and continued support over the last decade.

To everyone else involved – you know who you are – Biffa says Cheers!

Mike Bolam

Author's note: The term 'competitive match' is used throughout this book as describing Football League, Premiership, FA Cup, League Cup and European games only. Other competitions including Northern League, War Leagues, Anglo-Italian, Anglo-Scottish and Texaco Cups are not included unless stated.

All stats in *The Newcastle Miscellany* are correct up until the start of the 2007/08 season.

Foreword
By Les Ferdinand

I'm delighted to write the introduction to this book, which is full of facts, records and stories about Newcastle. I'm sure that fans of all ages will enjoy reading it.

The two years I spent at Newcastle were probably the most successful part of my career. We were winning most weeks and, in football, if you're winning more games than you're losing it all makes for a much more enjoyable experience. The whole city was involved in the club's success. There was a feelgood factor in Newcastle which made it an amazing place to be for those two years.

From day one, when a load of cheering fans turned up to greet me, the supporters made me feel welcome and that continued right up to the day I left. And it's no different when I go back to Newcastle now. A lot of the fans tell me I'm an adopted Geordie.

I know it's been said before, but Newcastle is a massive club. The support the team generates is just incredible. When I was playing at St James' Park the place was sold out every week with 36,000 season ticket holders. If they'd had the space, the club could have filled the place twice over. I used to bump into people before the match who told me they didn't have a ticket, they just used to come along and stand outside the ground to hear the noise of the crowd. Then, even at the training ground we'd have about 500 fans watching training every day. It's things like that which show why, for me at least, Newcastle supporters are by far the most passionate in the country.

When I signed for the club Kevin Keegan gave me the number nine shirt, worn in the past by some of the club legends profiled in this book like Hughie Gallacher, Jackie Milburn and Malcolm Macdonald. That was a great honour for me, because I knew what the shirt meant, and still means, to the Geordies. I got off to a great start by scoring against Coventry on my debut, and I felt I was off and running. Not as good as Len Shackleton, though, who I now know scored six goals on his Newcastle debut in 1946!

That first season we came very close to winning the Premiership title. Losing out to Manchester United in the end was one of the biggest disappointments of my career. We played some great stuff before Christmas but in the New Year we never quite hit the same heights. We had a bit of a break at one point and we never really got back to playing the way we did at the start of the season.

In the summer of 1997 Alan Shearer joined us from Blackburn. Kevin Keegan told me that Alan would be arriving and I thought it was just what we needed. Then he hit me with the request to give Alan my number nine shirt which, knowing what it means to the Geordie support, I agreed to. The book mentions that there were reports in the press that I approached the Premier League to wear a special '99' shirt, but they weren't true. Kevin Keegan told me I could have any number I wanted but I just went to the kit man and asked him what numbers were available. He said '23' so I said I'd take it, but then the board insisted that I have a number between one and 11. In the end I got the number ten shirt which became available when Lee Clark moved to Sunderland.

Sadly, even with Alan, we again had to settle for second place in 1997 and since then the loyal Newcastle fans have had to endure another decade without a trophy – as the book mentions more than once, you have to go back to 1969 for the last bit of silverware the club won.

Like anyone who has had any association with the club and experienced how passionate the supporters are, I am willing Newcastle to have some success after all those years. The club and the supporters thoroughly deserve it. And given his track record, I can certainly see Newcastle winning something under Sam Allardyce. Fingers crossed.

Dipping in and out of this book, I've been reminded about a lot of things I already knew about the club and found out loads more I didn't know – like the fact that Newcastle's first foreign players were a pair of brothers from Chile and that wartime striker Albert Stubbins appeared on the cover of The Beatles album *Sgt Pepper*.

I know that Newcastle fans love anything to do with the club and I'm sure that they will get a lot of enjoyment from this cracking little book.

Les Ferdinand

— FROM EASTENDERS TO WEST END BOYS —

Football was first played at St James' Park in October 1880, with a team called Newcastle Rangers occupying the site – although they were to play no part in the creation of the side that went on to be named Newcastle United.

In November 1881, a team named Stanley were founded by the cricket club of the same name, playing on a pitch at Stanley Street, Byker. Eleven months later Stanley changed their name to Newcastle East End and incorporated another recently-founded local team, Rosewood. By 1886 East End were on the move again, this time further out into the Eastern suburbs of Newcastle on Chillingham Road.

Elsewhere in the city, meanwhile, August 1882 had seen the formation of another football club, Newcastle West End, by the cricket club of the same name, playing initially on the Town Moor before relocating near to the Great North Road in Jesmond three years later. Then in May 1886 West End acquired the lease of St James Park, which hadn't been regularly used since Rangers moved out to a site in Byker in 1882.

West End and East End were by now the biggest clubs on Tyneside and, having regularly faced each other in friendlies since their inception and in the Northern League from season 1889/90, became arch rivals. However it was East End who came to dominate both in footballing and financial terms, winning 2–0 and 3–0 at St James' Park in the league and FA Cup respectively in October 1891 and the return game 7–1 at their Heaton Junction ground the following February.

Within three months of that crushing derby defeat West End were declared insolvent. However, rather than lose St James' Park to football, they sportingly offered the lease to their biggest rivals. East End gratefully took them up, kicking off life at St James' Park with a friendly against Celtic in September 1892 watched by 6,000 supporters. Then on 9th December, a public meeting was held seeking agreement on a new name in a bid to increase interest amongst the Tyneside public, with Newcastle United being decided upon.

The rest is history . . . with Newcastle United accepting an invitation to join the Football League (one that East End had rejected the previous season) along with fellow new boys Liverpool, Woolwich Arsenal, Rotherham Town and Middlesbrough Ironopolis in Division Two for the 1893/94 campaign.

— CHAMPIONS! —

Newcastle United: Champions!

The fourth and most recent occasion on which Newcastle United were crowned top-flight champions came on Saturday April 23rd 1927, a 1–1 draw at West Ham United confirming title success with two games still to play.

Only 21 players were used by the Magpies all season, with goalkeeper Willie Wilson, left-back Frank Hudspeth and outside-left Stan Seymour appearing in all 42 games. Top scorer with 36 strikes from 38 appearances was Hughie Gallacher, the talented but temperamental Scottish striker who had controversially succeeded Hudspeth as club captain that season. Seasonal highlights included a 4–0 opening day success over Aston Villa on Tyneside, with Gallacher grabbing all the goals.

United hit top spot for the first time in mid-January after completing the double over Villa. The Magpies' nearest challengers Huddersfield were then beaten 1–0 at St James' Park on Good Friday, 24 hours before Spurs were dispatched 3–2 at the same venue.

Newcastle did take possession of the Football League trophy again in season 1992/93, when Barry Venison was presented with it before a 7–1 home win over Leicester City. By that point, however, the First Division was no longer the top flight of English football – the greater prize being promotion to the Premiership.

Divison One Table, 1926/27:

	P	W	D	L	F	A	Pts
Newcastle United	42	25	6	11	96	58	56
Huddersfield Town	42	17	17	8	76	60	51
Sunderland	42	21	7	14	98	70	49
Bolton Wanderers	42	19	10	13	84	62	48
Burnley	42	19	9	14	91	80	47
West Ham United	42	19	8	15	86	70	46
Leicester City	42	17	12	13	85	70	46
Sheffield United	42	17	10	15	74	86	44
Liverpool	42	18	7	17	69	61	43
Aston Villa	42	18	7	17	81	83	43
The Arsenal	42	17	9	16	77	86	43
Derby County	42	17	7	18	86	73	41
Tottenham Hotspur	42	16	9	17	76	78	41
Cardiff City	42	16	9	17	55	65	41
Manchester United	42	13	14	15	52	64	40
The Wednesday	42	15	9	18	75	92	39
Birmingham	42	17	4	21	64	73	38
Blackburn Rovers	42	15	8	19	77	96	38
Bury	42	12	12	18	68	77	36
Everton	42	12	10	20	64	90	34
Leeds United	42	11	8	23	69	88	30
West Bromwich Albion	42	11	8	23	65	86	30

— THEY CALL US NEWCASTLE UNITED —

"I still love United and follow them, still feel the same delight and agony as everyone else. Once black-and-white, always black-and-white."
Irving Nattrass, Newcastle player and fan

"Newcastle are the one side I stand up for when they score a goal. I supported them as a kid, when me and our Robert used to go every Saturday."
Jack Charlton, Newcastle manager and fan

"They may not have won a trophy for many, many years but still 50,000 Geordies pour into St James' Park every home game. Which other club can command that sort of following?"
Nolberto Solano, Newcastle player and honorary Geordie

"I was worried to death that no-one would turn up. Ten years is a long time. People forget."
A relieved **Jackie Milburn** speaking after 45,000 attended his testimonial match in 1967 – a decade after he had retired from playing

"I just know this fellow can be another Jackie Milburn to the supporters."
Manager **Joe Harvey** introducing his new signing Malcolm Macdonald in 1971

"It was horrible – it ripped my heart out. I didn't want to go, I'd never even thought about going. I was playing for my team, my club."
Tynesider **Steve Watson** following his transfer to Aston Villa

"My career was over when I finished at Newcastle. Emotionally I couldn't play anywhere else."
Glaswegian Geordie **Bobby Mitchell**

"I understand most of what is said to me – unless it's by Alan Shearer. Geordie is a different language to English!"
Laurent Robert's number nine nightmare

"I went to Newcastle, met the Geordies on the Quayside, went out in the pubs and drank their beer."
The Dog on the Tyne was all **David Ginola's**

"He understood the Geordies and gave them what they loved."
Philippe Albert sums up the special gift of Kevin Keegan

— SOME TYNE-WEAR FACTS —

- John Auld became the first player to move from Sunderland to Newcastle, in October 1896.
- December 1906 saw James Raine make the first move in the opposite direction.
- Only three players have scored for both sides in Tyne-Wear derby matches: Ivor Broadis, Bob McKay and 'Pop' Robson.
- The 11 goals netted by Jackie Milburn remains the best scoring return for Newcastle against the Wearsiders.
- Wearsider Kevin Dillon appeared on trial for his hometown club after leaving Newcastle, but wasn't retained.
- Mike Hooper was loaned to Sunderland by Newcastle but failed to make an appearance.
- Albert Stubbins and Jackie Milburn appeared for Sunderland in war-time football.
- Newcastle United players who have refused to sign for Sunderland include: John Anderson (refused to leave Newcastle), Jon Dahl Tomasson (chose Newcastle instead) and David Kelly (chose Newcastle instead but subsequently signed for Sunderland).

— NEWCASTLE LEGENDS: JACKIE MILBURN —

Wor Jackie

Commemorated in books, plays, statues and songs, 'Wor Jackie' enjoyed a lifelong association with Newcastle United and his legend lives on two decades after his death.

Born into a footballing family (which included second cousins Jack and Bobby Charlton), Milburn's reputation was forged in the black and white of Newcastle and, for many football fans, he came to symbolise the club like no other player before or since.

Milburn's Magpies association began in 1943 when, as a 19 year-old, he played two trial matches at St James' Park – scoring twice in the first then blasting home six second-half goals the following weekend. This demonstration of powerful and accurate shooting was a taste of things to come.

His home debut in a war-time match in August 1943 was marked with a goal scored with his first touch, but Milburn had to wait until an end to hostilities and the start of the 1945/46 season to make his competitive bow.

A season before Football League fixtures returned, his debut came in the FA Cup, staged that season over two legs to assist clubs financially. Two goals in a 4–2 win over Barnsley sent a 60,284 crowd away from Gallowgate happy – although a 0–3 second leg reverse at Oakwell ended any Wembley dreams.

Then manager George Martin was to have a profound effect on Milburn's career in 1947, moving him to centre forward from the wing and handing him the number nine shirt. The switch paid instant dividends with a hat-trick away at Bury and a haul of 20 league goals that season as the Magpies returned to Division One.

However, it's for Milburn's FA Cup final exploits that he is best remembered: netting twice against Blackpool in the 1951 final and scoring after 45 seconds against Manchester City in 1955 en route to collecting a third winner's medal.

Many contemporary observers choose the sixth round tie away at Portsmouth in March 1952 as his finest display, a game which featured a hat-trick of memorable strikes.

After having left Tyneside for Belfast club Linfield in 1957, Milburn returned to England three years later at the age of 36, and was greeted with a number of offers.

Amid interest from Stoke City and various Scottish sides came a call from Charlie Mitten – the then Newcastle boss. However, Milburn was denied the chance of a Toon comeback after the Football League refused to sanction a request to repay his player's insurance policy.

Turning down the job of Ashington player-manager, he took a similar position at Yiewsley in Middlesex and briefly, at Carmel College in Wallingford. Milburn then managed Ipswich Town but, after just 18 months in charge, returned to the north-east in 1962 to spend the next two decades reporting on Newcastle United for a Sunday newspaper.

A testimonial game followed in 1967, in front of over 45,000 fans, while 1981 saw him the unwitting subject of the popular TV show *This is Your Life*.

Sadly, lung cancer claimed Jackie Milburn in October 1988. His funeral cortege fittingly slowed on Barrack Road, opposite St James' Park, en route to St Nicholas' Cathedral amid unprecedented numbers of mourners. Milburn's widow Laura later scattered his ashes across the Gallowgate End of the ground before returning to christen the stand that now bears his name.

Jackie Milburn factfile

Born: Ashington, May 11th 1924 Died: October 9th 1988
Newcastle career: 397 apps, 200 goals (1943–57)
Other clubs: Linfield
International: England, 13 caps, 10 goals

— ALL TIME PREMIERSHIP TABLE —

Despite having played one season fewer in the Premiership than ever-presents Aston Villa, Everton and Tottenham Hotspur, Newcastle United are statistically the fifth most successful Premiership side in the history of the competition:

Team	P	W	D	L	F	A	Pts
Manchester United	582	367	131	84	1,140	516	1,232
Arsenal	582	308	157	117	974	516	1,081
Chelsea	582	285	158	139	912	580	1,013
Liverpool	582	285	144	153	925	579	999
Newcastle United	**540**	**229**	**142**	**169**	**799**	**653**	**829**

— WHO THE **** ARE YOU? —

Current Football League sides that Newcastle have never faced competitively:

Accrington Stanley, Barnet, Boston United, Darlington*, Macclesfield Town, Milton Keynes Dons, Rochdale*, Wycombe Wanderers, Yeovil Town.

* Both faced in wartime football

— MIDDLE NAMES —

A selection of uncommon middle names that Newcastle United players have admitted to:

Robert **Sime** Aitken
Robert Francis **Dudgeon** Ancell
Anthony **Eugene** Cunningham
Amdy **Moustapha** Faye
John **Grattan** Hendrie
Frank **Calvert** Houghton
John **Bluey** Park
Alexander **Parrott** Ramsay
Glenn **Victor** Roeder
Kevin **Watson** Scott
William **Salmond** Thomson Penman

— TRUE COLOURS —

113 years of black and white stripes

"It was agreed that the Club's colours should be changed from red shirts and white knickers to black and white shirts (two inch stripe) and dark knickers."
Minutes of Newcastle United board meeting, August 1894

While there is no doubt about when Newcastle began to wear their familiar black and white striped shirts, the origins of that colour scheme remain in some dispute.

The club's inaugural season of league football in 1893/94 saw them appear in both the plain red shirt and white shorts and red and white striped shirts that their forerunners Newcastle East End had worn. Newcastle West End meanwhile had formerly appeared in a red and blue hooped shirt that was used as a basis for the change kit Newcastle United donned in the 1995/96 season.

Various suggestions have been made as to where the black and white colours originate from. One legend has it that the inspiration came from local clergyman, Father Dalmatius Houtman and his black and white uniform, another that there were some Magpies nesting in the ground around the time that the club changed its name. The most credible, however, suggests the black and white colours were copied from the Whitecoat army formed in the Tyneside area during the English Civil War. Favouring the Royalist cause, this army was established by the Cavendish family who were prominent local landowners and dressed their volunteer force in white shirts and dark trousers, boots, belts and hats.

Newcastle's appearance in black and white stripes was pre-dated by Notts County, who adopted that design a decade after being founded in 1880. Those other Magpies are also widely credited with being the inspiration behind Juventus adopting the colour scheme in 1903 after a member of the Italian club returned from England with a set of County strips.

Other Football League teams to have played in a black and white 'home' kit include New Brompton (who later became Gillingham), Rochdale, Grimsby Town and Watford.

— ST JAMES' PARK INTERNATIONALS —

Despite being initially selected as a venue for the 1966 World Cup Finals, wrangles over ground ownership and redevelopment between the club and Newcastle City Council saw the Football Association withdraw their hosting invitation in 1964. Middlesbrough's Ayresome Park was chosen to host three group stage ties instead, which were attended by the lowest crowds of the whole competition.

However, St James' Park has hosted various other senior international fixtures:

Date	Fixture	Competition
March 18th 1901	England 6 Wales 0	Home International
April 6th 1907	England 1 Scotland 1	Home International
November 15th 1933	England 1 Wales 2	Home International
November 9th 1938	England 4 Norway 0	Home International
June 10th 1996	Romania 0 France 1	Euro Championship
June 15th 1996	Bulgaria 1 Romania 0	Euro Championship
June 18th 1996	France 3 Bulgaria 1	Euro Championship
September 5th 2001	England 2 Albania 0	World Cup Qualifier
August 18th 2004	England 3 Ukraine 0	Friendly International
March 30th 2005	England 2 Azerbaijan 0	World Cup Qualifier

The stadium has also been earmarked as one of six UK venues to host the football tournament at the 2012 Olympics.

— CARELESS WHISPERS —

Among a myriad of transfer rumours involving Newcastle, certain non-moves have reached urban myth status:

Jimmy Greaves. Writing in his 2003 autobiography, the former England striker claimed that he turned down an illegal transfer approach from a Newcastle director in 1959. Despite being offered more than double his Chelsea salary, Greaves refused to leave Stamford Bridge – neither he nor his wife Irene fancying a move up north.

Ronnie Glavin. According to the local press, Barnsley's goalscoring midfielder was allegedly on the brink of a move to Tyneside on countless occasions in the late 1970s. He never left Oakwell.

Sócrates. The famed Brazilian midfielder was linked with a move to Tyneside from Corinthians in the early 1980s – the (fictional) justification being that the Doctor of Medicine and Philosophy graduate was coming to study at Newcastle University.

Roberto Baggio. Fans and media men at St James' Park for the press conference announcing the signing of Les Ferdinand spotted a black and white shirt with the name 'Baggio' on the back seat of a car parked outside the ground. The shirt was quickly revealed to be a wind-up perpetrated by director Douglas Hall.

However, it subsequently came to light that a United delegation had recently flown to Italy to speak to Baggio's agent, only to fail to agree financial terms. Within days, the player moved from Juventus to AC Milan.

— THERE'S NO PLACE LIKE HOME . . . PARK —

The longest possible journey between English football league stadia remains the 820–mile round trip between Newcastle and Plymouth.

To date, there have been 33 competitive meetings between the two sides, the Magpies having made 17 pilgrimages to Devon between 1905 and 1991. And on top of the long distance involved, the two most recent two trips to Home Park presented extra problems for the travelling contingent.

December 1990 saw the Division Two fixture scheduled for a noon start on a Sunday – Argyle being reluctant to cancel their lucrative Christmas shopper park and ride scheme based at the stadium car park! A crowd of 7,845 attended.

One year on and another Yuletide fiasco saw travelling Newcastle fans faced with making the journey for a game staged on the Friday evening before Christmas. Only 5,048 fans bothered to show up, including no more than 200 away supporters.

— WMD: WITNESS TO MAGPIE DECEPTION? —

Nowhere has the rise in respectability of football among the chattering classes been more evident than in the political arena, where club affiliations that were once hidden are now worn as a badge of honour. That has inevitably led to some dubious attempts at claiming allegiance – none more so than in the case of one Anthony Charles Lynton Blair. Allegedly.

Speaking in a Radio 5 interview in December 1997, the then-Prime Minister is famously said to have revealed his bogus Newcastle-supporting credentials. In particular, critics and political opponents seized on the fact that he claimed to have sat on the Gallowgate End as a youngster to watch Jackie Milburn play.

Unfortunately for the PM, that part of the ground was all standing until 1994 and 'Wor Jackie' made his final Newcastle appearance in 1957, when young Tony was four years old – and living in Australia.

Routinely trotted out as a prime example of Blair's manufactured personality, it took until 2005 for this popular myth to be tested and then promptly dispelled. An investigation by BBC's *Newsnight* programme uncovered the original tape of the interview and confirmed that it differed from subsequent newspaper reports of it – the latter being the widely-quoted source rather than the former. Absent from the tape are references to sitting or standing at the Gallowgate End or any area of St James' Park, while Blair revealed his Magpies affiliation to have begun "just after Jackie Milburn".

It's beyond suggestion though that the former Prime Minister may be implicated in any 'cash for honours' scandal – at least involving his favourite football club. One look in the St James' Park trophy cabinet should be enough to prove that.

— BEFORE WE WERE SO RUDELY INTERRUPTED —

One immediate effect of Britain's formal declaration of war against Germany on September 3rd 1939 was the immediate suspension of competitive football fixtures. That meant that the opening games of the 1939/40 season were expunged from the records, including Newcastle's three games in Division Two:

Date	Result
August 26th 1939	Millwall 3 Newcastle United 0
August 30th 1939	Nottingham Forest 2 Newcastle United 0
September 2nd 1939	Newcastle United 8 Swansea Town 1

Lost to history therefore are the goals scored at St James' Park in an 8–1 win over Swansea Town on the last Saturday before war was declared – a hat-trick from Ray Bowden, two from Tommy Pearson and efforts from David Hamilton, Willie Scott and Billy Cairns.

When the Football League programme resumed after the war, the 1939/40 fixture list was resurrected, with United fairing rather better the second time round:

Date	Result
August 31st 1946	Millwall 1 Newcastle United 4
September 5th 1946	Nottingham Forest 0 Newcastle United 2
September 7th 1946	Newcastle United 1 Swansea Town 1

Appearing in both the opening game of 1939 and 1946 against Millwall at St James' Park were no fewer than five players: Tom Swinburne, Benny Craig, Duggie Wright, Jimmy Woodburn and Tommy Pearson. Of the other six Magpies who played in the 1939 Swansea Town game, five resumed their careers with various clubs after the end of hostilities. Bowden, however, never played competitive football again.

— KNOT FOR THE FAINT-HEARTED —

Gallows humour still thrives at St James' Park

In recent years the southern end of St James' Park has been officially christened The Newcastle Brown Ale South Stand – even though the adjacent brewery is now closed. However to traditionalists it will always be 'The Gallowgate End', so named as it was built on the route from Newcastle's New Gate Gaol to the site of the town's gallows.

The last public execution at the gallows took place in 1844, less than 40 years before football was being played on the same site. On that occasion, a death sentence was served on Mark Sherwood of nearby Blandford Street for the murder of his wife.

Indeed Newcastle was synonymous for its big crowds long before a football was ever kicked at St James' Park. In 1829, more than 20,000 people turned up to witness the hanging of a notorious female murderer.

The exact site of the gallows is believed to have been adjacent to Leazes Terrace, on the site of what is now the East Stand.

— FAIRS CUP GLORY —

Famously, the last major trophy won by Newcastle United was the Fairs Cup of 1969. But exactly how Newcastle ended up in the competition that season is a story in itself.

The Inter Cities Fairs Cup was the precursor to the UEFA Cup, with the original 1955 rules admitting into the competition a single representative team for each city that organised trade fairs. That pretty soon fell by the wayside in favour of a one club per city entry policy.

When Newcastle ended the 1967/68 season in tenth place of Division One, this rule worked spectacularly in their favour. Champions Manchester City were joined in the European Cup by runners-up and holders Manchester United, third-placed Liverpool and fourth-placed Leeds United entering the Fairs Cup. The one-club, one-city rule excluded Everton in fifth spot, but admitted Chelsea in sixth as England's third Fairs Cup side, representing London. Tottenham Hotspur and Arsenal both therefore missed out as a result, despite finishing in seventh and ninth positions respectively.

And when ninth-place finishers West Bromwich Albion beat Everton in the FA Cup Final to take a spot in the European Cup Winner's Cup competition, the fourth and final Fairs Cup place was Newcastle's.

Had the result been reversed and Everton won the FA Cup, the Toffees would have gone into the Cup Winners' Cup and West Brom would have taken the final Fairs Cup place rather than Newcastle. So, indirectly, the man Magpies fans have to thank for their Fairs Cup triumph is West Brom striker Jeff Astle, scorer of the only goal in the 1968 FA Cup Final.

— PREMIERSHIP RECORD —

By the end of the 2006/07 season Newcastle United had played 540 Premiership games, winning 229 of those, drawing 142 and losing 169.

	Played	Won	Drawn	Lost
Home:	270	156	63	51
Away:	270	73	79	118

In these games the Magpies have scored 799 goals and conceded 653.

— TWIN TOWERS PART I —

One year after the famous 'White Horse Final' of 1923, Newcastle made their first appearance at the new Empire Stadium — with both players and supporters finding it rather to their liking. Here are the club's results at Wembley up to and including Newcastle's last FA Cup win in 1955:

April 27th 1924   FA Cup Final   Won 2–0 against Aston Villa
Newcastle team: Bradley, Billy Hampson, Frank Hudspeth, Edward Mooney, Charlie Spencer, Willie Gibson, James Low, Willie Cowan, Neil Harris, Tommy McDonald, Stan Seymour.
Scorers: Seymour, Harris.

April 23rd 1932   FA Cup Final   Won 2–1 against Arsenal
Albert McInroy, Jimmy Nelson, David Fairhurst, Roddie Mackenzie, Dave Davidson, Sammy Weaver, Jimmy Boyd, Jimmy Richardson, Jack Allen, Harry McMenemy, Tommy Lang.
Scorer: Allen (2).

April 28th 1951   FA Cup Final   Won 2–0 against Blackpool
Jack Fairbrother, Bobby Cowell, Bobby Corbett, Joe Harvey, Frank Brennan, Charlie Crowe, Tommy Walker, Ernie Taylor, Jackie Milburn, George Robledo, Bobby Mitchell.
Scorer: Milburn (2).

April 3rd 1952   FA Cup Final   Won 1–0 against Arsenal
Ronnie Simpson, Bobby Cowell, Alf McMichael, Joe Harvey, Frank Brennan, Ted Robledo, Tommy Walker, Bill Foulkes, Jackie Milburn, George Robledo, Bobby Mitchell.
Scorer: G. Robledo.

May 22nd 1955   FA Cup Final   Won 3–1 against Manchester City Ronnie Simpson, Bobby Cowell, Ron Batty, Jimmy Scoular, Bob Stokoe, Tommy Casey, Len White, Jackie Milburn, Vic Keeble, George Hannah, Bobby Mitchell.
Scorers: Milburn, Mitchell, Hannah.

A local newspaper reporter described the crowd's reaction to Jackie Milburn's second goal in 1951 as follows:

"The Geordies seemed to want to jump right into Heaven. The spectacle was a study of mass delirium, a black and white sketch of mass hysteria in its most nerve-shattering form."

— NEWCASTLE LEGENDS: LEN WHITE —

Yorkshire grit in black and white

Newcastle's failure to appear in a third successive FA Cup Final in 1953 had one silver lining, Len White being signed from Rotherham just days after he had inspired the Millers to a 3–1 fourth round victory at Gallowgate.

The 22-year-old Yorkshireman cost £12,500 and spent the early part of his Newcastle career operating on the right flank, while still working as a miner at Burradon Colliery.

However, White's reputation as one of the best uncapped players of the era was built on his performances for the Magpies at centre forward after the departures of Jackie Milburn and Vic Keeble.

A run of stylish free-scoring displays made White a genuine crowd favourite, although inconsistency elsewhere in the side often meant that his efforts up front were nullified by defensive lapses.

White's sole honour was a 1955 FA Cup Winner's medal – a game in which he delivered the corner for Jackie Milburn to head home against Manchester City in the opening seconds at Wembley. Untimely cup exits at the hands of the likes of Millwall and Scunthorpe United were to follow in subsequent seasons, though, while his haul of 22 goals in 30 league appearances in 1957/58 was only enough to see the club narrowly avoid relegation.

Had White played for a London club, an England call-up would have been likely. As it was though, his appearance for a Football League XI in November 1958 gave a hint of what his country missed. Playing against an Irish League side at Anfield, White scored three goals in eight second-half minutes during a 5–2 victory.

However, like Tony Green a decade later, injury was to overshadow White's career. A challenge by Tottenham's Dave Mackay at White Hart Lane in March 1961 took the gloss off a 2–1 victory against the team who would complete the Double within weeks. Sidelined for six months with ruptured ankle ligaments, by the time White returned to the Magpies line-up they were in Division Two and manager Charlie Mitten was about to be jettisoned, as his side struggled to mount a promotion bid.

It was evident that the injury had robbed White of his pace and in February 1962 he returned to his native Yorkshire, joining Huddersfield as the makeweight in a deal which took Scottish forward Jimmy Kerray to St James' Park.

After being belatedly rewarded for his efforts for the club with a testimonial game in 1989 (held at Whitley Bay after Newcastle United scandalously refused to take part), cancer claimed White in 1994 at the age of 64.

While Jackie Milburn remains synonymous with United's 1950s achievements, Len White is something of a forgotten hero.

Len White factfile
Born: Skellow, March 23rd 1930   Died: June 17th 1994
Newcastle career: 270 apps, 153 goals (1953–62)
Other clubs: Rotherham, Huddersfield, Stockport County

— IT'S A KNOCKOUT —

While no TV coverage of the FA Cup would be complete without footage of 'that' Ronnie Radford goal from 1972, the 'Nightmare on Edgar Street' is by no means the only occasion on which the Magpies have exited from the competition at the hands of lower league opposition.

In the 50 seasons since the resumption of the competition in 1946, United have been humbled by supposedly inferior sides on no fewer than 19 occasions – 11 of those coming in front of disbelieving crowds on Tyneside:

Season	Opponent	Score	Feat
1948/49	Bradford Park Ave (h)	0–2	Division 3 beat Division 1
1956/57	Millwall (a)	1–2	Division 3 South beat Division 1
1957/58	Scunthorpe United (h)	1–3	Division 3 North beat Division 1
1960/61	Sheffield United (h)	1–3	Division 2 beat Division 1
1961/62	Peterborough (h)	0–1	Division 3 beat Division 2
1963/64	Bedford Town (h)	1–2	Non-League beat Division 2
1967/68	Carlisle United (h)	0–1	Division 2 beat Division 1
1971/72	Hereford United (a)	1–2	Non-League beat Division 1
1972/73	Luton Town (a)	0–2	Division 2 beat Division 1
1974/75	Walsall (a)	0–1	Division 3 beat Division 1
1977/78	Wrexham (a)	1–4	Division 3 beat Division 1
1979/80	Chester City (h)	0–2	Division 3 beat Division 2
1980/81	Exeter City (a)	0–4	Division 3 beat Division 2
1985/86	Brighton and Hove Albion (h)	0–2	Division 2 beat Division 1
1988/89	Watford (a)	0–1	Division 2 beat Division 1
1991/92	AFC Bournemouth (h)	3–4	Division 3 beat Division 2 (on pens)
1993/94	Luton Town (a)	0–2	Division 1 beat Premier League
2002/03	Wolverhampton Wanderers (a)	2–3	Division 1 beat Premiership
2006/07	Birmingham City (h)	1–5	Championship beat Premiership

— SING IN THE . . . —

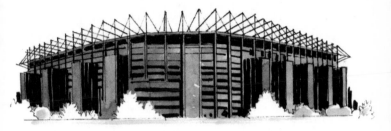

St James' Park

As St James' Park has been altered over the years, so have the names of different parts of the stadium. Here's a bluffer's guide to the Toon's ground:

North

Now known as the 'Sir John Hall Stand', this end of the ground will forever be the 'Leazes End' to diehard black and whiters. Once the home to the most vocal supporters, the covered standing terrace was closed and bulldozed following the home game against Manchester City in March 1978.

In its place came a reduced size uncovered terrace and the retaining walls for a stand that wasn't actually constructed until 1993.

Season 1986/87 saw temporary seating installed, with reconstruction of the West Stand meaning season ticket holders were relocated to an uncovered stand borrowed from a motor racing circuit (hence its unofficial name of the 'Silverstone Stand').

South

Currently labelled 'The Newcastle Brown Ale South Stand', this is more commonly referred to as 'The Gallowgate End' (although club literature in the early 1990s unsuccessfully attempted to label it 'The City End'). This part of the ground is also known as 'The Scoreboard', after the electronic boards installed there in the 1980s and 1990s and earlier manual efforts. The reconstruction of the stadium saw an all-seater covered stand opened in 1994, with sections linking the stand to the constructions adjoining to the East and West Stands following soon after.

East

Although the East Stand has been in place for over 30 years, this side of the ground is still referred to by some as the 'Popular Side', a reference to the former open terrace that stood here and ran the length of the pitch. Also now gone but still mentioned occasionally are 'The Benches' – seats at were installed at the front of this stand following an incident in 1980 when a firebomb was thrown into the travelling West Ham United supporters in the north-east corner. These were removed in the early 1990s when the stand was remodelled and the original executive boxes relocated to the West side of the ground.

West

For decades the only seated accommodation available (with the best seats in the 'Centre Pavilion'), the West Stand was demolished at the end of the 1986/87 season and replaced by a new construction christened 'The Milburn Stand'. Later alterations during the 1990s saw the standing areas that remained in front of the original reconstruction seated, removing the distinct 'Wing Paddocks' (A & E) and 'Centre Paddock' sections.

Corners

The north-east corner of the ground is nicknamed 'Firebomb Corner' – a reference to the previously mentioned events of March 1980. Reconstruction of the West Stand saw the dressing rooms sited in portakabins behind the Leazes End during season 1987/88, with the north-east corner closed to supporters in order to allow the teams to access the field via this section. The south-east corner of the ground is routinely referred to as 'The Corner' or 'The Strawberry Corner' – the latter after the adjacent pub of that name.

— DOUBLE RATIONS —

The once traditional scheduling of League fixtures on both Christmas Day and Boxing Day last saw Newcastle United in action on December 25th and 26th back in 1957.

On Christmas Day Nottingham Forest visited Tyneside and triumphed 4–1 in front of 25,214 spectators. United gained revenge, though, 24 hours later on the banks of the Trent, winning 3–2 at the City Ground watched by a crowd of 32,359.

Some fixtures were scheduled on December 25th in both 1958 and 1959 before the practice was finally discontinued. However, Newcastle didn't have games on Christmas Day in either season.

— LEAGUE OF NATIONS —

By the end of the 2006/07 season, no fewer than 129 players from 36 different countries had represented Newcastle United in their 14 seasons of Premiership football:

Country	Player Total
England	56
France	13
Scotland	8
Republic of Ireland	7
Wales	5
Northern Ireland	3
Argentina	2
Greece	2
Italy	2
Netherlands	2
Nigeria	2
Portugal	2
Spain	2

Plus single representatives from: Australia, Belgium, Brazil, Canada, Chile, Colombia, Croatia, Cyprus, Czech Republic, Denmark, Democratic Republic of Congo, Georgia, Germany, Norway, Paraguay, Peru, South Africa, Senegal, Sweden, Switzerland, Trinidad and Tobago, Turkey and the United States of America. Of those 129 players, 24 came through the ranks from the Newcastle United Academy.

* International affiliation rather than country of birth has been taken as a measure, for example Alan Neilson was born in Germany but played for Wales. Four players have also made Premiership appearances for the club in separate spells – Tommy Wright, Robbie Elliott, Lee Clark and Pavel Srnicek. These players are only counted once in the above totals.

— LET THERE BE LIGHT —

Newcastle United were only the third First Division club to install floodlights. The lights were switched on for a friendly against Celtic in February 1953 . . . and promptly switched-off again during the half-time interval, plunging the entire crowd into darkness.

The lights illuminated the first-ever floodlit FA Cup tie between two league sides, although Newcastle was not one of them. The match in question was a first round replay between Carlisle and Darlington on November 28th 1955.

— NEWCASTLE LEGENDS: SHAY GIVEN —

Shay Given: already a Toon legend

Shay Given celebrated a decade with Newcastle United in May 2007, having been bought from Blackburn for £1.5 million by his former Rovers boss Kenny Dalglish. Dalglish had first spotted the goalkeeper's potential when he was a teenager at Celtic, signing Given for Blackburn in 1994.

Having being loaned to both Swindon Town and Sunderland (who it was rumoured were unable to fund a permanent transfer), Given tussled with Steve Harper for the position of first-choice goalkeeper at St James Park for a number of seasons.

The Irish international took pole position in the 2000/01 campaign, missing just four Premiership fixtures as he established himself in the side after withdrawing a hastily submitted transfer request.

During that season, Given began a run of 140 consecutive Premiership appearances at Leeds in January 2001, making 100 per cent appearance records in the following three seasons. That impressive run was broken in October 2004 when Given remained on Tyneside as his wife gave birth – Steve Harper deputising away at Bolton.

By the end of the 2006/07 season, Given had risen to sixth in Newcastle's all-time appearance table (see *International Appearances*, page 26) and with a contract keeping him on Tyneside until 2011, he has a great chance of becoming the first Magpie ever to reach the 500 mark.

An outstanding shot-stopper, Given's importance to Newcastle was recognised by then manager Glenn Roeder when he was appointed captain following the retirement of Alan Shearer in the summer of 2006. Shortly after taking the skipper's armband, however, Given was involved in a sickening collision at West Ham United in September 2006 which left him with abdominal injuries that the surgeon who operated on him likened to those suffered by car crash victims. He returned to action after two months to put in some excellent performances, but ended another season having seen his efforts undermined by the shortcomings of those players in front of him.

Like all goalkeepers, Given has had a few moments he would prefer to forget – none more so than the goal he conceded against Coventry at Highfield Road in November 1997. In an initially innocuous piece of play, Given claimed possession of the ball on the edge of his six-yard box and threw the ball down in front of him in preparation for clearing it downfield. However, as a number of reporters later wryly observed, he was the only Irishman who didn't know where Dublin was – Coventry striker Dion Dublin appearing from behind him and scoring a perfectly legitimate goal by tapping the loose ball into the Newcastle net.

A far better memory for Given was being awarded the captain's armband by Ireland boss Steve Staunton in March 2007, leading his side out at Dublin's Croke Park against Slovakia. That honour came on the occasion of Given's 80th full international cap, which equalled the previous Ireland record for a goalkeeper, held by Packie Bonner.

For consistency, few in the modern game can match Given's record. If, as he must fear, he emulates Alan Shearer's trophy-free stint on Tyneside it would be a poor return indeed for his years of loyal service.

Shay Given factfile
Born: April 20th 1976, Lifford, County Donegal
Newcastle career: 413 apps (1997–)
Other clubs: Celtic, Blackburn Rovers, Swindon Town (loan), Sunderland (loan)
International: Republic of Ireland, 80 caps

— TWIN TOWERS PART II —

Venue of Legends for some, Wembley Stadium has proved to be nothing but an arena of misery for Newcastle supporters since the club's last success there in 1955. As Alan Shearer commented in 2002, "for Newcastle United, the sooner they knock down this place the better".

May 4th 1974   **FA Cup Final**   **Lost 0–3 to Liverpool**
Newcastle team: Iam McFaul, Frank Clark, Alan Kennedy, Terry McDermott, Pat Howard, Bobby Moncur, Jimmy Smith (Tommy Gibb), Tommy Cassidy, Malcolm Macdonald, John Tudor, Terry Hibbitt.

February 28th 1976   **League Cup Final**   **Lost 1–2 to Manchester City**
Mick Mahoney, Irving Nattrass, Alan Kennedy, Stewart Barrowclough, Glen Keely, Pat Howard, Mickey Burns, Tommy Cassidy, Malcolm Macdonald, Alan Gowling, Tommy Craig. Substitute unused: Paul Cannell.
Scorer: Gowling.

August 11th 1996   **FA Charity Shield**   **Lost 0–4 to Manchester United**
Pavel Srnicek, Steve Watson, Darren Peacock, Philippe Albert, John Beresford, David Batty, Robert Lee, Peter Beardsley (Tino Asprilla), Alan Shearer, Les Ferdinand, David Ginola (Keith Gillespie). Substitutes unused: Shaka Hislop, Warren Barton, Steve Howey, Lee Clark, Paul Kitson.

May 16th 1998   **FA Cup Final**   **Lost 0–2 to Arsenal**
Shay Given, Stuart Pearce (Andreas Andersson), Steve Howey, Nicos Dabizas, Alessandro Pistone, Gary Speed, David Batty, Robert Lee, Alan Shearer, Temuri Ketsbaia (John Barnes), Warren Barton (Steve Watson). Substitutes unused: Shaka Hislop, Philippe Albert.

May 22nd 1999   **FA Cup Final**   **Lost 0–2 to Manchester United**
Steve Harper, Andy Griffin, Laurent Charvet, Nicos Dabizas, Didier Domi, Robert Lee, Didi Hamann (Duncan Ferguson), Gary Speed, Alan Shearer, Temuri Ketsbaia (Glass), Nolberto Solano (Silvio Maric). Substitutes unused: Shay Given, Warren Barton, Stephen Glass.

April 9th 2000   **FA Cup Semi-final**   **Lost 1–2 to Chelsea**
Shay Given, Warren Barton, Steve Howey, Nicos Dabizas, Aaron Hughes (Temuri Ketsbaia), Robert Lee, Gary Speed, Kieron Dyer, Alan Shearer, Duncan Ferguson (Didier Domi), Nolberto Solano. Substitutes unused: Steve Harper, Alain Goma, Diego Gavilan
Scorer: Lee.

— TRANSFER TRAIL I —

In chronological order, Newcastle United's record purchases have been as follows:

Player	Year	Fee	Paid to
Bobby Templeton	1903	£400	Aston Villa
Andy McCombie	1904	£700	Sunderland
George Wilson	1907	£1,600	Everton
Billy Hibbert	1911	£1,950	Bury
Neil Harris	1920	£3,300	Partick Thistle
Hughie Gallacher	1925	£6,500	Airdrieonians
Jack Hill	1928	£8,100	Burnley
Harry Clifton	1938	£8,500	Chesterfield
Len Shackleton	1946	£13,000	Bradford Park Avenue
George Lowrie	1948	£18,500	Coventry City
Jimmy Scoular	1953	£22,250	Portsmouth
Ivor Allchurch	1958	£28,000	Swansea Town
Barrie Thomas	1962	£45,000	Scunthorpe United
Wyn Davies	1966	£80,000	Bolton Wanderers
Jimmy Smith	1969	£100,000	Aberdeen
Malcolm Macdonald	1971	£180,000	Luton Town
Peter Withe	1978	£200,000	Nottingham Forest
John Trewick	1980	£250,000	West Bromwich Albion
Paul Goddard	1986	£415,000	West Ham United
Mirandinha	1987	£575,000	Palmeiras
John Robertson	1988	£750,000	Heart of Midlothian
Dave Beasant	1988	£850,000	Wimbledon
Andy Thorn	1988	£850,000	Wimbledon
Andy Cole	1993	£1,750,000	Bristol City
Ruel Fox	1995	£2,225,000	Norwich City
Darren Peacock	1995	£2,700,000	Queens Park Rangers
Les Ferdinand	1995	£6,000,000	Queens Park Rangers
Tino Asprilla	1996	£7,500,000	Parma
Alan Shearer	1996	£15,000,000	Blackburn Rovers
Michael Owen	2005	£16,000,000	Real Madrid

— INTERNATIONAL APPEARANCES —

The current holder of the club's international appearance record is Shay Given, who broke the record on April 30th 2003 when playing for the Republic of Ireland against Norway.

A clean sheet that night in a 1–0 win at Lansdowne Road marked the 50th senior cap of the goalkeeper's career and the 41st earned whilst a Newcastle player. In doing so he broke the previous 40 game tally of Northern Ireland's Alf McMichael – a record that had stood for some 43 years.

Since then, Given has extended the record further, reaching 80 caps for Ireland (and therefore 71 as a Magpie) in March 2007. And McMichael's tally was also subsequently bettered by Greek defender Nicos Dabizas and Northern Ireland's Aaron Hughes.

Newcastle United's top ten international appearance makers:

Rank	Player	Total	Country
1	Shay Given	71	Republic of Ireland
2	Nicos Dabizas	43	Greece
3	Aaron Hughes	41	Northern Ireland
4	Alf McMichael	40	Northern Ireland
5	Gary Speed	36	Wales
6	Alan Shearer	35	England
7	Kieron Dyer	32	England
8	Nolberto Solano	28	Peru
9=	Peter Beardsley	25	England
9=	David Craig	25	Northern Ireland
10	Dick Keith	23	Northern Ireland

Note: Only caps gained whilst a Newcastle player are included in this list.

— SHOOT-OUT FAILURES —

Before beating Watford on penalties in the League Cup 2006, Newcastle had lost all seven of their previous competitive shoot-outs:

Year	Opponent	Competition
1971	Pecsi Dozsa	Inter-Cities Fairs Cup
1979	Sunderland	League Cup
1992	AFC Bournemouth	FA Cup
1996	Chelsea	FA Cup
1998	Blackburn Rovers	League Cup
2002	Everton	League Cup
2003	Partizan Belgrade	Champions League Qualifier

— NEWCASTLE LEGENDS: MALCOLM MACDONALD —

Supermac!

One of the finest strikers in Newcastle's illustrious history, Malcolm Macdonald was signed from Luton Town in 1971 for £180,000 by Toon boss Joe Harvey to solve a goalscoring problem.

Arriving at St James' Park in a hired Rolls Royce exuding brashness and confidence, Macdonald had a similar swagger on the pitch. In his five years on Tyneside he scored many memorable goals, beginning with a hat-trick against Liverpool on his home league debut. Fast and powerful, Macdonald possessed an explosive left foot and many of his best strikes – like his rocket shot at home to Leicester City that has gone down in folklore as one of the best ever seen at Gallowgate – gave the opposition keeper absolutely no chance of making a save.

The goals kept on coming, but the writing was on the wall for Macdonald when Harvey was replaced by Gordon Lee, a cautious manager who advocated a strict 'no stars' policy. Relations between club and player soon deteriorated, with an eventual parting of the ways coming in August 1976 when Arsenal shelled out £333,333 to take him to Highbury.

On the field, a parallel can be drawn between Macdonald and his eventual successor in the number nine shirt Alan Shearer. Both were to leave Newcastle without winners' medals or goals in either of their two cup final appearances. However, both enjoyed some happy moments in the semi-finals that led to those Wembley appearances, Macdonald scoring twice against Burnley in 1974 at Hillsborough in front of a fevered Newcastle support.

While Shearer's public image remains spotless and his managerial prowess untested, the same cannot be said for Macdonald. His early career in management at Fulham showed signs of promise before disintegrating in the fall-out from a controversial game with Derby County that blighted hopes of promotion for the Cottagers. Later, in an eight-month spell at Huddersfield, his side was on the wrong end of a confidence-shattering 10–1 league defeat away at Manchester City. After his management career ended, Macdonald experienced a number of setbacks in his business and personal life and for a while was a self-confessed alcoholic.

Happily, he has now recovered and has developed a new career as a talk-in pundit and radio chat show host in the north-east.

Malcolm Macdonald factfile
Born: Fulham, January 7th 1950
Newcastle career: 228 apps, 121 goals (1971–76)
Other clubs: Fulham, Luton Town, Arsenal
International: England, 14 caps, 6 goals

— GOLD STANDARD —

Eighteen players have appeared in World Cup finals while their registration was held by Newcastle United. They are:

Year	Host	Player	Nation
1950	Brazil	Jackie Milburn	England
1950	Brazil	George Robledo	Chile
1954	Switzerland	Ivor Broadis	England
1958	Sweden	Tommy Casey	Northern Ireland
1958	Sweden	Dick Keith	Northern Ireland
1958	Sweden	Alf McMichael	Northern Ireland
1986	Mexico	Peter Beardsley	England
1986	Mexico	David McCreery	Northern Ireland
1986	Mexico	Ian Stewart	Northern Ireland
1990	Italy	Roy Aitken	Scotland
1998	France	David Batty	England
1998	France	Robert Lee	England
1998	France	Alan Shearer	England
2002	Japan/South Korea	Kieron Dyer	England
2002	Japan/South Korea	Diego Gavilan	Paraguay
2002	Japan/South Korea	Shay Given	Republic of Ireland
2006	Germany	Michael Owen	England
2006	Germany	Craig Moore	Australia

In addition, Stephane Guivarc'h officially signed for Newcastle 24 hours after becoming a World Cup winner with France in 1998. The striker made his sixth appearance of the tournament in the final against Brazil, but failed to score in any of them. His lack of form attracted the attention of TV pundits including a certain Ruud Gullit, who was somewhat disparaging. Little did Gullit know though that within a matter of weeks he would be Guivarc'h's manager at St James' Park.

— TRADESMAN'S ENTRANCE —

With the traditional post-career profession of public house landlord having been superseded by media pundit or player's agent, here's a selection of slightly more individual ways in which former Newcastle United players have earned a crust after hanging up their boots:

Player	Profession
Philippe Albert	Market trader (fruit and vegetables)
Martin Burleigh	Painter and decorator
Andy Hunt	Adventure travel host in Belize

Albert Bennett	Joke shop proprietor
Ralph Callachan	Taxi driver
Tommy Casey	Fishmonger
Mick Channon	Racehorse trainer
Tony Cunningham	Solicitor
Bill Curry	Window cleaner
Billy Day	On-course bookmaker
Ed Dixon	Cinema manager
Pat Heard	Illusionist (stage name: Patrick Stewart)
William Hughes	Fisherman
Bill Imrie	Butcher
James Jackson	Blacksmith
Tom Philippson	Lord Mayor (of Wolverhampton)
Eric Ross	Travel agent
Willie Scott	Lollipop man
Scott Sloan	Fireman
George Thompson	Sign writer

— LONDON CALLING —

Saturday 2nd September 1893 saw both Newcastle United and Woolwich Arsenal play their first-ever Football League fixtures, the sides meeting at the Manor Ground in Plumstead, South East London.

However it proved to be a testing debut in the capital for the team from Tyneside who had arrived at Kings Cross by train early on the morning of the game having been unable to afford hotel accommodation.

The teams lined up as follows:

Woolwich Arsenal: Williams, Powell, Jeffrey, Devine, Buist, Howat, Gemmell, Henderson, Shaw, Elliott, Booth.

Newcastle United: Ramsay, Jeffrey, Miller, Crielly, Graham, McKane, Bowman, Crate, Thompson, Sorley, Wallace.

With Newcastle trailing at the interval to a Shaw effort, Arsenal quickly doubled the lead through Elliott. However goals from Tom Crate and Jock Sorley gave Newcastle a point (some contemporary reports crediting Willie Graham as scoring Newcastle's opener).

— SHEAR CLASS —

Alan Shearer is the Premiership's highest ever scorer, closely followed by one Andrew Cole. In fact, four of the Premiership's top scorers have notched a fair few of their tally in the black and white stripes off Newcastle United.

Premiership Top Ten Goalscorers:

Player	Total	For Newcastle
Alan Shearer	260	148
Andrew Cole	188	43
Thierry Henry	174	–
Robbie Fowler	162	–
Les Ferdinand	149	41
Teddy Sheringham	147	–
Jimmy Floyd Hasselbaink	127	–
Michael Owen	125	7
Dwight Yorke	122	–
Ian Wright	113	–

— SHOOT-OUT TRIUMPH —

An instantly forgettable 2006/07 season for Newcastle United was memorable for one achievement – the breaking of a competitive penalty shoot-out hoodoo that had extended over 35 years.

November 7th 2006 saw the Magpies in League Cup fourth round action at Premiership rivals Watford. But after 90 minutes of normal time and an extra half hour left the two sides locked at 2–2, Newcastle faced their eighth competitive penalty shoot-out – having lost the previous seven. With Nolberto Solano stepping up to take the first kick, here's how history was made:

Newcastle:			Watford:		
Solano	scored	1–0	Henderson	scored	5–1
Milner	saved	1–1	Young	missed	1–1
Emre	scored	2–1	Spring	scored	2–2
Duff	scored	3–2	Bangura	scored	3–3
Carr	scored	4–3	Bouazza	scored	4–4
N'Zogbia	scored	5–4	Stewart	saved	5–4

Goalkeeper Steve Harper saved the 12th spot-kick to deny Jordan Stewart, before celebrating with the travelling fans behind him in the Vicarage Road Stand.

— NEWCASTLE LEGENDS: ALAN SHEARER —

Shearer, Shearer!

It is something of a minor tragedy that Alan Shearer ended his career with a single honour, the Premiership winner's medal he collected with Blackburn Rovers.

A one-time schoolboy trialist with Newcastle – contrary to urban myth he only played briefly in goal during his trial – Shearer began his professional career at Southampton before making a big money move to Blackburn in 1992. At Ewood Park his forceful centre forward play and powerful shooting were key factors in the Lancashire side's 1995 title success. However, a year later, after spurning offers from Manchester United, Arsenal and Barcelona, Shearer was persuaded by Kevin Keegan to return to his Geordie roots.

Twenty five goals in 31 Premiership games earned a second successive runner's up spot for his new club, despite the shock mid-season departure of his teenage hero Keegan (a young Shearer can be seen acting as ball boy in footage of Keegan's testimonial).

His second season at the club began badly when he was seriously injured in a pre-season tournament at Goodison Park in August 1997.

He returned to action to fire the club into successive FA Cup finals in 1998 and 1999, only to end up on the losing side on both occasions.

Despite his goals and clear commitment to the Newcastle cause, both Ruud Gullit and Sir Bobby Robson subsequently attempted to dislodge Shearer from his perch as the uncrowned King of Tyneside – the former by controversially leaving him out of the side against Sunderland, the latter attempting to sell him to Liverpool.

Shearer outlasted both managers, though, and postponed his planned retirement after talks with their successor Graham Souness in 2005. His decision to carry on playing enabled him to set a new Newcastle scoring record. Goal number 200 against Mansfield Town in the FA Cup at St James' Park in January 2005 equalled Jackie Milburn's tally and a month later he claimed the record outright against Portsmouth.

Shearer's goals during this period helped another new manager – caretaker boss Glenn Roeder – to a winning start, amid widespread speculation that Roeder was merely keeping the seat warm for the popular Magpies' skipper.

A revitalised Newcastle rose into the top half of the table in the second half of the 2005/06 season, with a trip to Sunderland giving Shearer more reason to celebrate as he helped his side come from behind by scoring goal number 206.

However, within ten minutes of scoring from the spot, Shearer's playing career was over – caught accidentally in the tackle by Julio Arca and forced off with medial knee ligament damage. The injury meant he missed the remaining three games of the season – although he was able to make a cameo appearance in a farewell testimonial at Gallowgate against Celtic. Shearer appeared for kick-off before leaving the field, returning in the final seconds to sign off by converting a penalty with typical aplomb.

Proceeds from the sell-out game, merchandising and other events eventually totalled £1.64 million – which was donated to various charitable causes.

A regular BBC pundit, Shearer is also now working towards his UEFA 'A' Licence coaching qualification, having enrolled on a course run by the Scottish Football Association.

Medals may have eluded Shearer during his Newcastle career, but the pleasure he provided from his goalscoring exploits remains undiminished. Only he knows though whether he has unfinished business at Gallowgate.

Alan Shearer factfile
Born: Gosforth, August 13th 1970
Newcastle career: 404 apps, 206 goals (1996–2006)
Other clubs: Southampton, Blackburn Rovers
International: England, 63 caps, 30 goals

— TWELFTH NIGHT —

- Albert Bennett holds the distinction of being the first ever Newcastle United substitute, following a change in the rules at the start of the 1965/66 season allowing teams to name a twelfth man (although the sub was only allowed to come onto the pitch to replace an injured player). Consequently, Bennett remained firmly seated on the bench during the Magpies' 2–2 draw with Nottingham Forest at St James' Park on August 21st 1965.

- The honour of being Newcastle's first playing sub went to Ollie Burton on September 4th 1965 when he replaced Trevor Hockey (who had sustained a shin injury) during a 2–0 home victory over Northampton Town. And it was Burton who became the first Newcastle player to net after coming on to the field as a substitute, scoring in a 1–2 defeat to Lincoln City at Sincil Bank in the Football League Cup on September 13th 1967.

- On August 29th 1987 the number of substitutes permissible was raised to two, with the Magpies first using their number 12 and 14 in a 0–1 home loss to Nottingham Forest. On that occasion Kenny Wharton and Paul Goddard gave way to John Anderson and Andy Thomas.

- Three substitutes were permitted for the first time at the start of the 1995/96 season, with then-manager Kevin Keegan making a trio of replacements for the first time in the sixth Premiership game of the season, the visit of Manchester City to Tyneside. In a 3–1 victory for United on September 16th 1995, Warren Barton gave way to Steve Watson, Scott Sellars replaced John Beresford and Ruel Fox was introduced for Peter Beardsley.

- The first-ever substitute to be appear back in the 1965/66 season was Keith Peacock of Charlton Athletic. His son Gavin later played for Newcastle United.

— WEAR SO HAPPY —

Saturday April 5th 1980 wasn't a great day for the travelling Newcastle fans among a 41,752 crowd at Roker Park. A Stan Cummins goal settled the 115th Wear-Tyne derby and ultimately helped propel Sunderland to a second place finish in Division Two. However, in 11 trips to Wearside since that defeat up to the start of the 2007/08 season Newcastle have lost none of them:

Season	Score	Newcastle scorer(s)	Crowd
1984/85	0–0		28,246
1989/90	0–0		29,499
1989/90	0–0		26,641
1991/92	1–1	Liam O'Brien	29,224
1992/93	2–1	Liam O'Brien, Gary Owers (own goal)	28,098
1996/97	2–1	Peter Beardsley, Les Ferdinand	22,037
1999/00	2–2	Helder, Didier Domi	42,192
2000/01	1–1	Andy O'Brien	48,277
2001/02	1–0	Nicos Dabizas	48,290
2002/03	1–0	Nolberto Solano (penalty)	45,067
2005/06	4–1	Michael Chopra, Alan Shearer (penalty) Charles N'Zogbia, Albert Luque	40,032

Games up until the 1996/97 season were staged at Roker Park. Since then, the fixture has been played at the Stadium of Light. The Red and Whites have beaten the Magpies at their new ground, but only at reserve level!

— #9 DREAM PART I —

Although the so-called 'Summer of Love' didn't really have much of an impact on Tyneside, Newcastle fans can still claim a (slightly tenuous) link to the record that what was for many the soundtrack of the psychedelic era.

On June 1st 1967 The Beatles released *Sgt Pepper's Lonely Hearts Club Band* on the Parlophone label – an album routinely cited as one of the most innovative and inspirational pieces of popular music ever recorded.

As well as the ground-breaking material though, much attention was also focused on the cover artwork, which consisted of the 'Fab Four' plus a montage of more than 70 iconic personalities that The Beatles themselves had chosen.

These appeared in life-size cardboard cut-out form – a concept originally devised by Paul McCartney, designed by Peter Blake, created by art director Robert Fraser and photographed on March 30th 1967 by Michael Cooper.

Included among the various world leaders, entertainers, philosophers and poets were three sportsmen – boxer Sonny Liston, Olympic swimmer Johnny Weissmuller and former Liverpool centre forward Albert Stubbins (Everton legend William Ralph 'Dixie' Dean was also considered but not included).

Born in Wallsend, Stubbins had moved to Liverpool from Newcastle in 1946, rapidly becoming a Kop favourite and playing for the Anfield club until 1953. His place in the montage has variously been claimed to have been at the urging of both John Lennon and Paul McCartney, the former allegedly because Stubbins was a great favourite of his father Fred Lennon. McCartney also seems to have been a Stubbins fan, later sending him a telegram: "Well done Albert for all those glorious years in football. Long may you bob and weave."

Regardless of whose choice it was, a photo of a grinning Albert in his Liverpool strip can be seen towards the centre of the group – just behind Marlene Dietrich.

In 2003, the International Federation of the Phonographic Industry (IFPI), certified that worldwide sales of *Sgt Pepper's* . . . had exceeded 32 million – that's an awful lot of Alberts . . .

— FAMILIAR FACES —

On the final day of the 2006/07 season Shay Given moved up another place in the all-time Newcastle United appearances list when he returned from injury to play Watford.

The goalkeeper had begun the campaign outside the top ten, but despite several enforced absences now has a top four place in his sights – and may yet become the first Newcastle player to break the 500-game barrier.

The top ten competitive appearance makers for the club are:

Rank	Player	Total	Timespan
1	Jimmy Lawrence	496	1904–1922
2	Frank Hudspeth	472	1910–1929
3	Frank Clark	457	1962–1975
4	Bill McCracken	432	1904–1923
5	Alf McMichael	431	1949– 1963
6	Shay Given	413	1997–
7	David Craig	412	1962–1978
8	Bobby Mitchell	408	1949–1961
9	Alan Shearer	404	1996–2006
10	Jackie Milburn	397	1946–2006

— NEWCASTLE LEGENDS: PETER BEARDSLEY —

Time fails to dim the brilliance of Peter Beardsley's finishing

Spotted playing youth football on Tyneside, Peter Beardsley had trials at Gillingham, Cambridge United, Burnley and Newcastle United without earning a professional contract. For a while it seemed the talented but lightweight schemer would have to consider a career outside football.

Fortunately for Beardsley, former Magpies captain Bob Moncur got wind of his abilities and talked the 18 year-old into playing for his Carlisle United reserve side at Newcastle Blue Star in 1979. Beardsley scored that night in a 3–2 win at the Wheatsheaf and quickly agreed terms with the Brunton Park club, where he continued to earn rave reviews.

In 1981 he moved to the North American Soccer League with Vancouver Whitecaps but two years later joined Arthur Cox's Newcastle side after a brief one-game flirtation with Manchester United.

Beardsley helped Newcastle to promotion in his first season with the club but after Cox was replaced by Jack Charlton, he found himself competing for a place up front with burly forwards Tony Cunningham and George Reilly. Under new manager Willie McFaul, Beardsley was back in favour, but he grew increasingly frustrated with a perceived lack of ambition at the club.

In July 1987 he departed for Liverpool in a record £1.9 million deal, and remained on Merseyside for a six-year spell which included two seasons at Everton. It was during this period that Beardsley won the bulk of his 59 England caps, forming a successful forward partnership with Gary Lineker.

In 1993, Kevin Keegan brought Beardsley, now aged 32, back to Tyneside. Using his exceptional close ball skills to supply the prolific Andy Cole when he wasn't scoring sensational goals himself, he was a prime mover in establishing Newcastle United back in the top flight.

After leaving Newcastle for a second time in 1997, he took in stops at Bolton Wanderers, Manchester City, Fulham, Hartlepool and Doncaster Rovers.

A sell-out testimonial game at St James' Park in 1999 saw his boyhood favourites Celtic come to town, the occasion featuring the likes of Kenny Dalglish, Andy Cole and Kevin Keegan back in black and white for one night. None of these stars were surprised to learn that Beardsley, one of the most enthusiastic footballers of his generation, had played for Hartlepool's first team the evening before his big night.

For those who saw this skilful, creative and clever player at his peak certain memories are embedded. Among the most vivid moments are the chip over Brighton goalkeeper Joe Corrigan on the final day of the 1983/84 season, a New Years' Day hat-trick at home to Sunderland in 1985, and from his second spell, superb late winners at White Hart Lane and Selhurst Park. Time fails to dim the brilliance of his finishing.

Even after his retirement from senior football, Beardsley has continued to entertain and delight Newcastle fans with his annual appearance in the 'Masters' Indoor Football tournament.

Peter Beardsley factfile
Born: Longbenton, January 18th 1961
Newcastle career: 324 apps, 119 goals (1983–87 and 1993–97)
Other clubs: Carlisle United, Vancouver Whitecaps, Manchester United, Liverpool, Bolton Wanderers, Manchester City (loan), Fulham, Hartlepool United, Doncaster Rovers, Melbourne Knights
International: England, 59 caps, 9 goals

— SHEARER STATS —

Some number-crunching in honour of Newcastle United's record goalscorer:

Shearer's overall league record:
Alan Shearer career record (Premiership/Div1): 558 games, 283 goals
Alan Shearer career record (all comps): 733 games, 379 goals

By club:

Southampton	140 starts (18 as substitute)	43 goals
Blackburn Rovers	165 starts (6 as substitute)	130 goals
Newcastle United	395 starts (9 as substitute)	206 goals

By season:

Season Club	Games (League)	(all)	Goals (League)	(all)
1987/88 Southampton	5	5	3	3
1988/89 Southampton	10	10	0	0
1989/90 Southampton	26	35	3	5
1990/91 Southampton	36	48	4	14
1991/92 Southampton	41	60	13	21
1992/93 Blackburn Rovers	21	26	16	22
1993/94 Blackburn Rovers	40	48	31	34
1994/95 Blackburn Rovers	42	49	34	37
1995/96 Blackburn Rovers	35	48	31	37
1996/97 Newcastle United	31	40	25	28
1997/98 Newcastle United	17	23	2	7
1998/99 Newcastle United	30	40	14	21
1999/00 Newcastle United	37	50	23	30
2000/01 Newcastle United	19	23	5	7
2001/02 Newcastle United	37	46	23	27
2002/03 Newcastle United	35	48	17	25
2003/04 Newcastle United	37	51	22	28
2004/05 Newcastle United	28	42	7	19
2005/06 Newcastle United	32	41	10	14

Note: Alan Shearer's 63 full England caps and 30 goals are not included in these figures.

— OOPS! —

Toon-related radio and TV commentary foul-ups include:

Rodney Marsh

The former Fulham, Queens Park Rangers, Manchester City and England footballer found himself out of a job in January 2005 after an on-air joke backfired on him.

During the live phone-in programme *You're on Sky Sports*, Marsh commented that: "David Beckham would never move to Newcastle because of all the trouble caused by the Toon Army in Asia."

Coming just weeks after the devastating tsunami tidal wave was estimated to have claimed 300,000 lives, reaction was swift and Marsh's contract was torn up. A Sky Sports spokesman said: "These remarks should never have been made and Sky would like to offer its apologies to those who were offended."

Marsh himself said: "I am hugely disappointed in myself for letting them down. I apologise unreservedly for any offence I caused by my thoughtless and inappropriate comment I made last night. My intention was to make a light-hearted football joke."

Ian Payne, radio reporter

"Tomorrow, the whole of Newcastle versus Manchester United."

Tom Tyrrell, radio reporter

"Newcastle are finally going to end their London bogey. They haven't won there since . . . a long time ago. That would be a ghost . . . no an albatross off their necks."

Jim White, Sky Sports presenter

"Michael Owen to Newcastle is the biggest transfer of the season so far – and it will be until there's a bigger one."

Brian Moore, TV presenter

"Alongside me is Keggy Keegle, sorry Kevin Keegle."

Ian St John, Channel 5 pundit

During an advert break before the Croatia Zagreb versus Newcastle Champions League qualifier in 1997, St John passed the time by picking his nose. Unfortunately for him he failed to realise that the cameras were still rolling – and his nasal explorations were being beamed live on the scoreboard at the Maksimir Stadium.

— THE NAME NOW LEAVING
FROM PLATFORM NINE —

The name of Newcastle United once adorned the sides of a railway locomotive – but only the most keen-eyed would ever have seen it for themselves thanks to some apparent skulduggery on the part of the London and North Eastern Railway.

Often referred to as the 'Footballer Class', the B17 class of locomotives were designed by Sir Herbert Nigel Gresley, with 73 built at various locations between 1928 and 1937; 25 of which were given the names of English football clubs.

No. 2858 rolled out of Darlington Works on May 28th 1936 resplendent in green livery and with a nameplate incorporating a brass football, black and white decoration and the name 'Newcastle United'.

However, when the locomotive appeared at a railway exhibition in Romford just ten days later, it bore nameplates proclaiming it to be 'The Essex Regiment' – a name it carried until it was withdrawn from operating service and scrapped in December 1959.

The reasons for the change of heart were never fully explained, although club rivalries may have played some part in the decision. In the event, the B17 class were never a common sight in the North East due to a lack of power.

It's presumed that the 'Newcastle United' nameplates were scrapped as they have never surfaced, but a replica nameplate was commissioned and presented to the club in 2003 by Magpies fan and railway enthusiast David Tyreman.

— 'THE PIRATE' —

Newcastle chairman between 1964 and 1978, Lord Westwood remains a controversial figure despite passing away in 1991.

Much of the blame for the stagnation of the club in the 1970s and a lack of investment in the team and stadium is laid at his door by commentators of the era. Westwood, who was popularly known as 'The Pirate' due to an eye patch that covered his right eye (the result of a car accident), resigned as chairman in 1978 and left the Board altogether in 1981 – refusing on both occasions to use his own funds to underwrite financial rescue packages.

A one-time president of the Football League, it was said of Westwood that he would swap his patch to cover his good eye when watching Newcastle lose.

— FANZINES —

August 1988 saw the publication of the first issue of *The Mag* – an unofficial fanzine composed and compiled by a small group of Newcastle fans and billing itself as an independent supporters' magazine

Priced at 50p and with a cover including a photograph of a young and trendily attired Paul Gascoigne, *The Mag* certainly wasn't short of targets to snipe at.

Issues covered in this debut copy included the enduring racist chanting at St James' Park and the unwelcome presence of National Front supporters selling their racist publication *Bulldog* outside the ground on matchdays.

Also the subject of grumbling was the continued lack of covered standing accommodation at the stadium, which at the time still had two open ends.

The threat from proposed new coverage of games on satellite TV was also mentioned, while the departure of Peter Beardsley earlier in the year to Liverpool – allegedly to fund the cost of constructing the Milburn Stand – was also discussed.

Fast forward to the end of the 2006/07 season and *The Mag* has enjoyed an uninterrupted run and reached issue number 217, just shy of 19 years since it first appeared.

A sister publication *True Faith* first appeared at the start of the 1999/00 season, taking a more left-field look at Toon-related events and providing a platform for those writing about football culture. By mid 2007, it had reached issue 58.

Various other unofficial Newcastle United fanzines have come and gone over the years, including:

Black and White
The Geordie Times
The Giant Awakes
Half Mag Half Biscuit
Jim's Bald Heid
The Mighty Quinn
The Number Nine
Oh Wi Ye Naa
Once Upon A Tyne
Talk of the Toon
Talk of the Tyne
Toon Army News

— CHALKED OFF? —

Newcastle United were involved in one of the most controversial incidents in the history of the FA Cup, when they faced Arsenal at Wembley in the 1932 final.

Arsenal took the lead in the 12th minute, but Newcastle equalised seven minutes before half-time with what *The Times* described as 'the most controversial goal in English football history'.

Chasing a ball down the line, Newcastle's Jimmy Richardson stretched to reach the ball and delivered a cross into Jack Allen to score. However, many in the stadium felt the ball had crossed the line before Richardson crossed it.

Allen struck again on 72 minutes to give his side the win and the distinction of being the first side ever to have come from behind to win a Wembley FA Cup final.

However some discontent among supporters and Arsenal officials was evident, with claims that the ball had gone out of play before the first goal strengthened by newspaper reports of the game and photographs which appeared to back up the claims. The incident even knocked Adolf Hitler's victory in the Prussian elections off the front page.

And the conviction that there had been a miscarriage grew the following week when British Movietone News footage of the goal was shown in cinemas that purported to show that the ball was out of play via primitive freeze frame technology.

Invoking the spirit of future Gunners boss Arsene Wenger, Newcastle goalscorer Jack Allen told *The Guardian* newspaper: "From my position I could not see whether it had gone out of play or not."

While Richardson similarly claimed: "I was concentrating so hard on reaching the ball that I couldn't tell you whether it was over the line or not."

Match referee Percy Harper remained adamant, however: "I gave the goal in accordance with the rules and regulations of the Football Association – it was definitely a goal. The ball was definitely in play. I was so certain that the goal was good that I did not even consider it necessary to consult the linesman, and I am still just as certain. I was, of course, well up with the play, and was in a position to see the incident clearly. Whatever the film may appear to show will not make me alter my opinion."

— CELEBRITY FANS PART I —

A selection of celebrity supporters often associated with the club:

Ant and Dec
Geordie-born duo who have been present at games and kit launches etc since the early *Byker Grove* days and were on-field hosts for the Alan Shearer testimonial match in 2006.

Tony Blair
Former Prime Minister and MP for Sedgefield since 1983 (see *WMD: Witness to Magpie Deception?*, page 11).

Bryan Ferry
Popular singer, both with seventies band Roxy Music and as a solo artist.

Brendan Foster
Former distance runner who won Olympic Bronze and Commonwealth Gold medals before retiring and founding the Great North Run in 1981. Clad in a black and white vest, 'Big Bren' won a 3,000 metres challenge race round the Wembley pitch before the 1974 FA Cup Final between Newcastle and Liverpool. He had told the FA he would run in exchange for ten tickets to the match!

Robson Green
TV actor and St James' Park season ticket holder.

Steve Harmison
The Durham and England fast bowler is a season ticket holder and goes to away games when his cricketing commitments permit. (see *Magpies Cricket Club*, page 70)

Tim Healey
Comic actor who guested as stadium PA announcer before the Oxford United home game in 1992. Unfortunately, his slightly colourful repartee was never to grace the airwaves again.

Brian Johnson
Once the lead singer of Tyneside rock band, Geordie, Johnson's distinctive gravelly tones have been heard fronting mega-grossing heavy metallers AC/DC since 1980. A devoted fan, he played the part of an exiled Toon fan in the film *Goal* and once made an unsuccessful bid to join the Newcastle United board. His former wife Carol is now married to ex-Newcastle striker Malcolm Macdonald.

Mark Knopfler
Supremely talented guitarist and former member of Dire Straits. His instrumental composition 'Going Home' has become synonymous with the club in recent years –often called 'Local Hero' after the film soundtrack it appears on.

Gabby Logan
When known as plain Gabby Yorath (daughter of former Leeds and Wales star Terry), the TV presenter graduated from Durham University into a job on local radio, interviewing players on the touchline at St James' Park. She memorably wrote in *The Times* in April 2007 that:

"St James' Park is up there with the Bernabéu and the Nou Camp for atmosphere and grandeur. I will always love it — I can understand why people have their ashes spread on the pitch and why fans arrive at the ground three hours early. It's possible to appreciate other stadiums, for sure, but you'll only really ever love one."

John McCririck
Horse racing commentator and reality TV contestant.

— FULL SPEED AHEAD —

Gary Speed has made more appearances in the Premiership than any other player, with just under half of those coming in a Newcastle shirt.

Premiership Top Ten Appearance makers:

Player	Total	For Newcastle
Gary Speed	521	213
David James	476	–
Ryan Giggs	464	–
Alan Shearer	441	303
Gareth Southgate	426	–
Sol Campbell	422	–
Teddy Sheringham	418	–
Andy Cole	407	58
Ray Parlour	378	–
Robbie Fowler	372	–

— AND HERE'S TO BOBBY MONCUR —

It's a well-worn path to the banks of the Danube, striped goalposts and a funny shaped cup, but Newcastle's Fairs Cup success of 1968/69 remains the last bona fide trophy that the Magpies have won.

Beginning with a resounding home victory on the Magpies' European debut, five two-legged ties brought the club to a home and away final games against Hungarian side Ujpesti Dozsa:

Route to Glory:

Opponent	Score	Newcastle scorer(s)	Crowd
Feyenoord (h)	4–0	Scott, Robson, Gibb, Davies	46,348
Feyenoord (a)	0–2		45,000
Sporting Lisbon (a)	1–1	Scott	9,000
Sporting Lisbon (h)	1–0	Robson	53,747
Real Zaragoza (a)	2–3	Davies, Robson	22,000
Real Zaragoza (h)	2–1	Robson, Gibb	56,055
Vitoria Setubal (h)	5–1	Foggon, Robson, Davies, Robson, Gibb	57,662
Vitoria Setubal (a)	1–3	Davies	34,000
Rangers (a)	0–0		75,580
Rangers (h)	2–0	Scott, Sinclair	59,303
Ujpesti Dozsa (h)	3–0	Moncur 2, Scott	59,234
Ujpesti Dozsa (a)	3–2	Moncur, Arentoft, Foggon	34,000

Final line-ups:

May 29th 1969 St James' Park, Newcastle:
McFaul, Craig, Burton, Moncur, Clark, Gibb, Arentoft, Scott, Davies, Robson, Sinclair (Foggon) Substitutes unused: Hope, Craggs
Goal times: Moncur 63, 71, Scott 84

June 11th 1969 Megyeri Stadium, Budapest:
McFaul, Craig, Burton, Moncur, Clark, Gibb, Arentoft, Scott (Foggon), Davies, Robson, Sinclair. Substitutes unused: Hope, McNamee
Goal times: Moncur 46, Arentoft 53, Foggon 68 (For Ujpesti: Bene 30, Gorocs 43)

Across the 12 ties, Newcastle named 25 players, of whom four were on the field for every minute: Willie McFaul, Tommy Gibb, Wyn Davies and 'Pop' Robson. A further three – Ollie Burton, Frank Clark and Jimmy Scott – appeared in all 12 ties at some stage. The other 15 players utilised were: Geoff Allen, Benny Arentoft, Albert Bennett, John Craggs, David Craig, Keith Dyson, Dave Elliott, Alan Foggon, Ron Guthrie, Arthur Horsfield, Jim Iley, John McNamee, Bobby

Moncur, Jackie Sinclair and Graham Winstanley. Non-appearing goalkeeping substitutes Gordon Marshall, John Hope and Dave Clarke completed the squad.

— DOCTOR FEELGOOD —

When Michael Owen stepped on to the field at Reading's Madejski Stadium on 30th April 2007 after a ten-month absence through injury, Newcastle fans once again had cause to thank a 69-year-old native of Texas who has never seen a live Premiership football match.

The Steadman-Hawkins Clinic in Vail, Colorado, USA has hosted a steady stream of injured sportsmen and women including various golfers, tennis players and Olympic athletes.

A world-renowned Orthopaedics expert, Doctor Richard Steadman has performed over 10,000 operations in his career. However, it is for his work in curing career-threatening knee problems on a trio of Newcastle centre forwards – Alan Shearer, Craig Bellamy and Michael Owen – that Dr Steadman has become something of a hero to Toon fans. In addition, he also carried out a successful knee operation in 2001 on Leeds United striker Michael Bridges, who later signed for Newcastle.

The walls of Steadman's clinic are decorated with replica shirts signed by many of his grateful patients, as well as a signed photograph of Alan Shearer with the dedication: "Just when I was getting frustrated with the pain, you took it away. Many, many thanks."

And as well as the work carried out by Steadman, his colleague Doctor Marc Philippon has also done his bit for the black and white cause. The hip specialist carried out an operation on Newcastle striker Shola Ameobi, who had played on in discomfort for over two years before finally breaking down in September 2006.

Ameobi was playing again by April 2007 and also made his first-team comeback alongside Owen in Berkshire that night – watched by Dr Steadman over in the USA on satellite TV.

As Steadman said to Owen as he presented him with a DVD of his operation, "Whatever makes you retire from football, it won't be your knee."

Steadman the Magpie Healer, the complete record:

Player	Injury	Operation	Playing again
Alan Shearer	Right knee	January 2000	August 2001
Craig Bellamy	Right knee	April 2002	September 2002
Craig Bellamy	Left knee	October 2003	January 2004
Michael Owen	Right knee	July 2006	April 2007
Michael Owen	Right knee	September 2006	April 2007

— FOR FORK'S SAKE —

Having ended their four-year winless run in London at the 30th time of asking, Newcastle's players were entitled to feel pleased with themselves on December 19th 2001.

An eventful 3–1 win against Arsenal at Highbury had propelled Newcastle to the top of the Premiership. Unbeknown to them however, a higher power had been at work.

In the following day's *Evening Chronicle* cutlery-bending psychic Uri Geller described how he led the Spoon Army for one night:

"I knew the team would win. I am so happy for everyone who supports them. It was exactly what I said.

"I arrived late and had no ticket. But the moment I got out of the car and touched the Highbury stadium, the Arsenal player Ray Parlour was sent off.

"I started screaming and shouting for Newcastle to win. And soon after the start of the second half I said to my friend that Shearer would score from a penalty. That was half an hour before it happened. But I knew it. I knew the team would win. I am so happy for everyone who supports them. It was exactly what I said.

"While Newcastle were scoring their winning goals I was running round the outside of the ground 11 times to lift the hoodoo.

"I even predicted the 3–1 scoreline after I got to the ground. I sat in the car and listened to the game on the radio. And after Arsenal scored I decided it was time to act.

"There was a lot to do with the number 11. Newcastle had not won in 29 games and two plus nine is 11. Number 11 is very mystical and powerful. So I ran around the ground 11 times. The facts speak for themselves.

"I hope Newcastle will win the league but I have to concentrate and see. Right now I have done what you wanted.

"It is almost a guarantee the team will win when I have a moment to talk to the players in the dressing room, I wasn't able to do that last night but I was physically close to them which is important."

Despite Uri's powers, Newcastle failed to win the Premiership that season, ultimately finishing back in fourth, some 16 points behind champions Arsenal. And things got worse for Geller, with the Exeter City co-chairman seeing his "beloved" Grecians relegated into the Football Conference in 2003 – despite bringing his pal Michael Jackson to visit their St James Park ground.

— EDSON ENCOUNTER —

The end of the 1971/72 season saw Newcastle embark on an Asian tour, which included visits to Thailand, Hong Kong and Iran.

Providing the opposition in Hong Kong were the Brazilian side Santos, whose most famous player Edson Arantes do Nascimento (aka Pele) was in their line-up.

Newcastle led 2–1 at the interval thanks to a long-range effort from Tony Green and a John Tudor header – Pele at this stage having been virtually anonymous.

However, that all changed in the second half as Pele set to work, scoring a hat-trick in a devastating 15-minute spell that enthralled those fans present and ensured that Newcastle lost 2–4.

John Tudor recalled: "The delicate close-control skills, the amazing acceleration, the powerhouse shooting had the crowd in ecstasy. It was like trying to stop a flash of lightning."

His job done, Pele then left the field – pausing only to shake hands with the stunned Newcastle players.

— DREAM STARTS PART I —

Newcastle United players who scored a hat-trick or better on their competitive debut for the Magpies:

Year	Player	Opponent/venue	
1946	Len Shackleton	Newport County (h)	6 goals
1989	Mick Quinn	Leeds United (h)	4 goals
1926	Bob McKay	West Bromwich Albion (h)	3 goals
1935	Wilf Bott	Bury (h)	3 goals

Shackleton's debut came in an amazing 13–0 success in which his new team-mate Charlie Wayman (who scored four in the game) missed a penalty in the opening moments.

Coming in the days before television coverage and the FA's Dubious Goals Committee, 'Shack' was credited with his sixth and Newcastle's 13th, although Newport's Ken Wookey may have got the final touch. What isn't in doubt, however, is his incredible scoring rate, as he notched his second, third and fourth goals in this game within a 155-second period.

— IS THIS THE WAY TO . . . ? —

Current Football League stadia that Newcastle have never visited competitively:

Accrington Stanley (Fraser Eagle Stadium)*
Barnet (Underhill Stadium)*
Boston United (York Street Stadium)
Brighton and Hove Albion (Withdean Stadium)*
Bristol Rovers (Memorial Stadium)*
Chester City (Saunders Honda Stadium)
Coventry City (Ricoh Arena)*
Darlington (96.6 TFM DarlingtonArena)
Doncaster Rovers (Keepmoat Stadium)*
Hartlepool United (Victoria Park)
Huddersfield Town (Galpharm Stadium)
Hull City (Kingston Communication Stadium)
Macclesfield Town (Moss Rose)*
Millwall (The New Den)*
Milton Keynes Dons (National Hockey Stadium)*
Northampton Town (Sixfields Stadium)*
Rochdale (Spotland)
Scunthorpe United (Glanford Park)
Stoke City (Britannia Stadium)
Swansea City (The Liberty Stadium)*
Torquay United (Plainmoor)
Walsall (Bescot Stadium)
Wycombe Wanderers (Adams Park)*
Yeovil Town (Huish Park)

*Stadia yet to be visited at any level of football eg: friendlies, reserves etc. (up to start of 2007/08 season).

— NEWCASTLE'S TOP LEAGUE CUP SCORERS —

Player	Total
Malcolm Macdonald	12
Andy Cole	8
Alan Gowling	7
Alan Shearer	7
Gavin Peacock	5
Peter Beardsley	4
Craig Bellamy	4
Mickey Burns	4
Paul Cannell	4

— UPPERS AND DOWNERS —

Since Newcastle United first took their place in Division Two for the 1893/94 season, the club has enjoyed – and endured – no fewer than nine movements between the top two divisions in England.

Season	Move	Movers
1897/98	Promoted	Burnley, **Newcastle**
	Relegated	None
1933/34	Relegated	**Newcastle**, Sheffield United
	Promoted	Grimsby Town, Preston North End
1947/48	Promoted	Birmingham City, **Newcastle**
	Relegated	Blackburn Rovers, Grimsby Town
1960/61	Relegated	**Newcastle**, Preston North End
	Promoted	Ipswich Town, Sheffield United
1964/65	Promoted	**Newcastle**, Northampton Town
	Relegated	Wolverhampton Wanderers, Birmingham City
1977/78	Relegated	West Ham United, **Newcastle**, Leicester City
	Promoted	Bolton Wanderers, Southampton, Tottenham Hotspur
1983/84	Promoted	Chelsea, Sheffield Wednesday, **Newcastle**
	Relegated	Birmingham City, Notts County, Wolverhampton Wanderers
1988/89	Relegated	Middlesbrough, West Ham United, **Newcastle**
	Promoted	Chelsea, Manchester City, Crystal Palace*
1992/93	Promoted	**Newcastle**, West Ham United, Swindon Town*
	Relegated	Crystal Palace, Middlesbrough, Nottingham Forest

(*promoted via the Play-Offs)

Apart from the 1992/93 promotion, all of the above saw Newcastle move between Football League Divisions One and Two, the exception coming that season, when the Magpies moved from the renamed Division One to the Premier League.

— PACK OF THREE —

Hat-trick pioneers for the club:

First in Division Two: Willie Thompson in a 6–0 home win over Woolwich Arsenal on September 30th 1893.

First in Division One: Jock Peddie in an 8–0 home win over Notts County on October 26th 1901.

First in FA Cup: Bill Appleyard in a 5–1 home win over Grimsby Town on March 7th 1908.

First in Anglo-Italian Cup: Malcolm Macdonald in a 5–1 home win over Crystal Palace on May 21st 1973.

First in League Cup: Malcolm Macdonald in a 6–0 home win over Doncaster Rovers on October 8th 1973.

First in Premiership: Peter Beardsley in a 4–0 home win over Wimbledon on October 30th 1993.

First in UEFA Cup: Robert Lee in a 5–0 away win over Royal Antwerp on September 13th 1994.

First in Champions League: Faustino Asprilla in a 3–2 home win over Barcelona on September 17th 1997.

— WORLD OF SPORT —

Although it has been said that some of the performances served up at St James' Park have borne precious little resemblance to association football, there have been a range of other sports staged at the stadium since United moved in.

Miss Netty Honeyball and her British Ladies Football Club played an exhibition match in 1895, while the first of a number of baseball games were held in June 1918.

At other times, athletics meetings with both track and field events have taken place, along with cycling challenges. The stadium even hosted sheepdog trials in 1944, helping the war effort by raising funds for the adjacent Royal Victoria Infirmary. But perhaps the most famous non-football sports team to visit St James' Park were the Harlem Globetrotters, who made two appearances during the 1950s.

In latter years no additional sporting events have taken place on the field – with plans to relocate the Newcastle Falcons Rugby Union side being jettisoned when the decision to redevelop St James' Park rather than build a new stadium in Leazes Park was taken. However, the club-sponsored Lister Storm GT racing car did make an appearance before one game, painted in the black and white colours that it raced in at Le Mans in 1997.

— GONE FOR A BURTON —

On 15th April 1895 Newcastle played the final game of their second season in Division Two, with a tenth place finish assured. However, their away fixture against Burton Wanderers was to prove memorable for all the wrong reasons, as their Derby Turn ground proved to be venue for United's record defeat.

Trailing 0–4 at half time, the final score was 0–9 in favour of the home side, who avenged their 6–3 defeat on Tyneside earlier that season. For a team who had only managed four clean sheets in their previous 31 league and cup games that season, conceding goals wasn't a major shock to Newcastle and their porous defence.

The rigours of playing two home games in the three days running up to the Wanderers game may be a partial excuse. However, the following season saw all but two of the Newcastle side who appeared in the record defeat shipped out.

Some 38 years later, the Magpies 'celebrated' the anniversary of their record loss by slipping to a mere 1–6 defeat away to Leeds United.

— FAMILIAR FOES —

Since the two sides first met home and away within a few weeks of each other in September 1893 in Division Two, Newcastle United's most frequent competitive opponents have been Arsenal (known as 'Woolwich Arsenal' until 1914).

While St James' Park has remained the home venue for the Magpies throughout, Arsenal have moved twice since hosting Newcastle for the first time at their Manor Ground in Plumstead. A move across the Thames came in 1913, with Newcastle's debut at Highbury in August 1919 marked by a 1–0 away win. November 2006 then saw the Magpies visit the Emirates Stadium for the first time, a 1–1 draw being the outcome.

Newcastle's top ten most played opponents:

Opponent	P	W	D	L	F	A
Arsenal	159	65	35	59	227	219
Manchester City	157	70	37	50	240	210
Liverpool	155	45	38	72	193	261
Everton	152	61	32	59	228	221
Aston Villa	145	63	30	52	230	232
Manchester United	144	39	34	71	215	272
Chelsea	141	47	36	58	178	208
Tottenham Hotspur	137	50	30	57	202	216
Sunderland	137	50	44	43	207	206
Blackburn	131	55	29	47	201	191

— HOME FROM HOME —

Aside from St James' Park, the venue at which Newcastle have earned the most Premiership points is Villa Park. Here's the complete record of how and where the Magpies' have earned their points on the road since promotion in 1993.

Opposition	Frequency	Record	Pts
Aston Villa	14 visits	6 wins, 5 draws, 3 defeats	23
Leeds United	11 visits	6 wins, 3 draws, 2 defeats	21
Middlesbrough	11 visits	6 wins, 3 draws, 2 defeats	21
West Ham United	12 visits	5 wins, 2 draws, 5 defeats	17
Tottenham Hotspur	14 visits	5 wins, 1 draws, 8 defeats	16
Everton	14 visits	4 wins, 3 draws, 7 defeats	15
Sunderland	6 visits	4 wins, 2 draws, 0 defeats	14
Sheffield Wednesday	7 visits	3 wins, 3 draws, 1 defeats	12
Arsenal	14 visits	3 wins, 2 draws, 9 defeats	11
Coventry City	8 visits	3 wins, 2 draws, 3 defeats	11
Blackburn Rovers	12 visits	2 wins, 4 draws, 6 defeats	10
Derby County	6 visits	3 wins, 1 draws, 2 defeats	10
Leicester City	8 visits	2 wins, 4 draws, 2 defeats	10
Crystal Palace	3 visits	3 wins, 0 draws, 0 defeats	9
Charlton Athletic	8 visits	1 wins, 4 draws, 3 defeats	7
Ipswich Town	4 visits	2 wins, 1 draws, 1 defeats	7
Manchester City	9 visits	1 wins, 4 draws, 4 defeats	7
Birmingham City	4 visits	1 wins, 3 draws, 0 defeats	6
Bolton Wanderers	8 visits	2 wins, 0 draws, 6 defeats	6
Fulham	6 visits	2 wins, 0 draws, 4 defeats	6
Nottingham Forest	4 visits	1 wins, 3 draws, 0 defeats	6
Queens Park Rangers	3 visits	2 wins, 0 draws, 1 defeats	6
Southampton	12 visits	1 wins, 3 draws, 8 defeats	6
Liverpool	14 visits	1 wins, 2 draws, 11 defeats	5
Manchester United	14 visits	0 wins, 5 draws, 9 defeats	5
West Bromwich Albion	3 visits	1 wins, 2 draws, 0 defeats	5
Chelsea	14 visits	0 wins, 4 draws, 10 defeats	4
Wimbledon	7 visits	0 wins, 4 draws, 3 defeats	4
Norwich City	3 visits	1 wins, 0 draws, 2 defeats	3
Oldham Athletic	1 visits	1 wins, 0 draws, 0 defeats	3
Portsmouth	4 visits	0 wins, 3 draws, 1 defeats	3
Sheffield United	2 visits	1 wins, 0 draws, 1 defeats	3
Watford	2 visits	0 wins, 2 draws, 0 defeats	2
Barnsley	1 visits	0 wins, 1 draws, 0 defeats	1
Bradford City	2 visits	0 wins, 1 draws, 1 defeats	1

Swindon Town	1 visits	0 wins, 1 draws, 0 defeats	1
Wolverhampton Wanderers	1 visits	0 wins, 1 draws, 0 defeats	1
Reading	1 visits	0 wins, 0 draws, 1 defeats	0
Wigan Athletic	2 visits	0 wins, 0 draws, 2 defeats	0

— BLACK AND WHITE TV —

August 22nd 1964 saw the opening fixtures of the new football season and the debut of a new Saturday evening programme on BBC2, entitled *Match of The Day*. The debut transmission brought the nation highlights of the Division One match at Anfield, where reigning champions Liverpool overcame Arsenal 3–2.

Audience reaction was positive and within months the programme had branched out to cover the occasional lower league fixture. That policy brought fresh-faced young presenter Frank Bough and the cameras to a muddy Brisbane Road on February 20th 1965, to record Leyton Orient's home clash with Second Division leaders Newcastle United. Not for the last time though, Newcastle supporters endured a trial by TV, Joe Elwood netting twice for the Os to cancel out Ron McGarry's penalty.

The BBC then ignored the promoted Magpies in the following season, before covering them once again as they travelled to London in October 1966 – *Match of the Day* having by now graduated to BBC1. Unfortunately, things were little better, Arsenal beating the Toon at Highbury through a Michael Boot effort and a Frank Clark own goal.

A first visit by the cameras to St James' Park came two days before Christmas 1967, Newcastle earning a point in a 1–1 draw with Liverpool. Jimmy Scott scored for the Magpies, Ian St.John netting for the visitors.

Finally, after a televised 0–0 draw at Highbury in February 1968, Newcastle at last tasted victory in front of a nationwide TV audience for the first time on April 12th 1969, as a 'Pop' Robson penalty and Alan Foggon's strike accounted for Manchester United in front of an exuberant Tyneside crowd.

Newcastle's *Match of the Day* debut in colour came in September 1970, when two 'Pop' Robson goals were enough to beat West Ham at Upton Park.

— AWAY FROM THE NUMBERS —

As well as becoming professional footballers, a number of Newcastle United players have shown talent in other branches of sport, including:

Roy Aitken	Basketball
William Aitken	Sprinting
John Anderson	Gaelic Football
John Bailey	Boxing
Jimmy Boyd	Indoor Bowls
Jesse Carver	Weightlifting
David Edgar	Ice Hockey
Tommy Ghee	Water Polo
Chris Guthrie	Fly Fishing
Bobby Moncur	Yachting
Archie Mowatt	Cycling
Ron McGarry	Rugby League
Tommy Pearson	Golf
Jamie Scott	Pole Vaulting
Nigel Walker	Rugby Union
Ron Williams	Crown Green Bowls

— NO CUP OF CHEER —

Milk Cup or Littlewoods, Rumbelows, Coca Cola, Worthington or Carling Cup – call it what you like the 47-year history of the League Cup has been mostly miserable for the Magpies.

Although the competition was first staged in the 1960/61 season, Newcastle actually failed to register a victory until some three years later, a win over Preston North End halting a run of four defeats and two draws.

Of 117 ties played to the start of the 2007/08 season, in the club's complete League Cup gistory the Magpies have won 50 matches, drawn 19 and lost 48, scoring 181 times and conceded 154 goals (not including penalty shoot-outs).

Newcastle have both scored and conceded seven goals in a League Cup match: enduring a 2–7 reverse at Old Trafford against Manchester United in 1976 and registering a 7–1 success at Meadow Lane against Notts County in 1993.

NEWCASTLE
Home Kits
1881-2009

www.historicalkits.co.uk

1881 (East End)

1881 (West End)

1882-84

1894-97

1897-98

1903-04

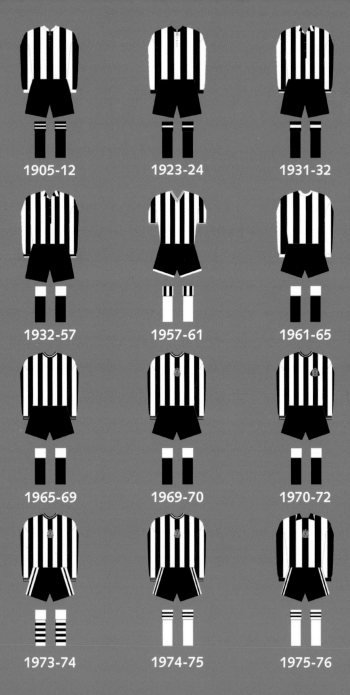

1905-12

1923-24

1931-32

1932-57

1957-61

1961-65

1965-69

1969-70

1970-72

1973-74

1974-75

1975-76

1976-78

1978-79

1980-83

1983-85

1985-86

1986-87

1987-88

1988-90

1990-91

1991-93

1993-95

1995-97

1997-99

1999-2000

2000-01

2001-03

2003-05

2005-07

2007-09

— THE WIT AND WISDOM OF
SIR BOBBY ROBSON —

"Tickets are selling like cream cakes"

"Rob Lee didn't have a number. Shearer was out of favour. There was no discipline. Players were going upstairs to eat whenever they wanted, using mobile phones whenever they wanted, the whole thing needed an overhaul."
Early days in the Newcastle job

"If we invite any player up to the Quayside to see the girls and then up to our magnificent stadium, we will be able to persuade any player to sign."
The attractions of Tyneside

"We can't replace Gary Speed. Where do you get an experienced player like him with a left foot and a head?"
A quick anatomy lesson

"If you see him stripped, he's like Mike Tyson. But he doesn't bite like Tyson."
Talking about Titus Bramble

"All right, Bellamy came on at Liverpool and did well, but everybody thinks that he's the saviour, he's Jesus Christ. He's not Jesus Christ."
Playing down the cult of Craig

"I handled Bellamy for four years. Graeme Souness couldn't stick four months."
More Craig claims

"We mustn't be despondent. We don't have to play them every week – although we do play them next week as it happens."
Having lost 2–0 to Arsenal, Newcastle prepared to face them in the FA Cup just days later.

"They can't be monks – we don't want them to be monks, we want them to be football players because a monk doesn't play football at this level."
Responding in somewhat bizarre fashion to criticism of player discipline

"When he gets his legs in tandem with his body, we'll make him a player."
On Shola Ameobi

"Tickets are selling like cream cakes."
Before a big match

"We didn't get the rub of the dice."
Mixing his metaphors

"There's a smell of the north-east which drew me back. I've got black and white blood and I'll stick at it because this is the team I love. I've got a big emotional feeling about it."
Smells like Toon Spirit, Bobby

"We are getting criticised for everything at the moment. There are knives going in my back and arrows flying around my head. But I don't think some people have any idea what we have had to do to keep the ship solvent."
Fighting for the Toon Army . . . the navy and the air force

"As for me, I still love it and I need it. I am more than ready for the challenge and I am determined to win at least one more trophy before I gallop off into the sunset."
Refuting retirement talk

"I say I'm almost over it but it will always rankle. I'll never forget what they did."
In unforgiving mood after his dismissal (1)

"I was kept in the dark with contracts and even transfers. Alex Ferguson, Arsène Wenger and Jose Mourinho know exactly what's going on at their clubs. That doesn't seem possible at Newcastle."
In unforgiving mood after his dismissal (2)

"My dad taught me the value of money and not to throw it away. My players have fame, adoration, money, women, fast cars and no mortgage ... in the real world, they'd be lucky to get £20,000 a year, never mind a week."
Telling his players a few home truths

— BLACK AND WHITE RIBBONS ON IT —

Despite failing to win the FA Cup since 1955, Newcastle remain inextricably linked with the world's oldest knockout competition.

Although both East End and West End had participated previously, Newcastle United made their FA Cup bow in January 1893, suffering a 2–3 home defeat at the hands of Middlesbrough.

Since that disappointing debut, the club have gone on to lift the trophy on six occasions, been beaten finalists seven more times and endured four unsuccessful appearances in the semi-finals.

However, the former final venue of Crystal Palace wasn't one that agreed with the Magpies, five visits to Sydenham in South London producing three defeats and two draws.

Final successes:

Season	Score	Opponent	Venue
1909/10	1–1	Barnsley	Crystal Palace, London
1909/10 (replay)	2–0	Barnsley	Goodison Park, Liverpool
1923/24	2–0	Aston Villa	Wembley
1931/32	2–1	Arsenal	Wembley
1950/51	2–0	Blackpool	Wembley
1951/52	1–0	Arsenal	Wembley
1954/55	3–1	Manchester City	Wembley

— NEWCASTLE LEGENDS: HUGHIE GALLACHER —

Hughie of the magic feet

Do you ken Hughie Gallacher the wee Scotch Lad?
The best centre forward Newcastle ever had
Contemporary children's rhyme

Having seen him net both goals for Scotland in an international match against England at Hampden Park in May 1925, Newcastle moved to sign Airdrieonians forward Hughie Gallacher.

However, it took the Magpies six months of protracted negotiations and a £6,500 transfer fee to land the diminutive but prolific 22-year-old goalscorer from Lanarkshire.

Gallacher netted twice on his debut in December 1925 as Newcastle drew 3–3 with Everton at St James' Park (Everton taking a point thanks to three goals from striker Dixie Dean, who Newcastle had attempted to sign before turning their attention to Gallacher).

Before leaving Tyneside in 1930, Gallacher gave the public four and a half goal-filled seasons – notching over 20 goals in each campaign he played in.

Captain of the side during the 1926/27 championship-winning

season, Gallacher's goals failed to bring further success to the club, and he fell foul of Newcastle's board of directors after a number of on-field clashes with both referees and opponents.

There was also the little matter of a colourful off-field lifestyle that saw him mix with supporters in local bars, dance halls and on occasion, Magistrates Courts.

After keeping a declining Newcastle side in the First Division, Gallacher was sold to Chelsea in May 1930 for £10,000 amid an outcry from supporters. A record attendance of almost 69,000 packed St James' to see Gallacher return with the Londoners in September of that year, although United's Jackie Cape deviated from the script by scoring the only goal of the game.

Gallacher was to return to Tyneside in 1938 after having appeared for Derby County, Notts County and Grimsby Town. He played one final season for Gateshead before settling in the town and holding down a variety of jobs, including a stint as a football writer.

And it was in Gateshead that he chose to take his own life, walking out in front of an approaching train in June 1957, having been called to appear in court to answer charges of maltreating his son.

Hughie Gallacher factfile
Born: Bellshill, north Lanarkshire, February 2nd 1903
Died: June 11th 1957
Newcastle career: 174 apps, 143 goals (1925–30)
Other clubs: Queen of the South, Airdrie, Chelsea, Derby County, Notts County, Grimsby Town, Gateshead
International: Scotland, 19 caps, 22 goals

— HOT SHOTS —

Newcastle United's top scorers in all competitive games:

Rank	Player	League	Cup	Total
1.	Alan Shearer	148	58	206
2.	Jackie Milburn	177	23	200
3.	Len White	142	11	153
4.	Hughie Gallacher	133	10	143
5.	Malcolm Macdonald	95	26	121
6.	Peter Beardsley	108	11	119
7.=	Bobby Mitchell	95	18	113
7.=	Tom McDonald	100	13	113
9.	Neil Harris	87	14	101
10.	Bryan 'Pop' Robson	82	15	97

— HUMAN BILLBOARDS —

The Magpies wore shirt advertising for the first time in 1980, with the Newcastle Breweries Blue Star logo appearing on the front of home and away shirts.

However, if match highlights were televised advertising was banned, so the presence of TV cameras at the opening day trip to Hillsborough saw Newcastle wearing unadorned yellow shirts.

The Blue Star debuted in a home draw with Notts County in August 1980, having also been worn at Gallowgate in a friendly against Leeds United earlier that month.

With shirt advertising still frowned upon by the FA, Newcastle were fined £1,000 for wearing strips with the logo in January 1981 against Sheffield Wednesday – even though the FA Cup tie wasn't televised.

Subsequent seasons saw the Blue Star continue to be used, until the brewer's deal expired at the end of the 1985/86 season.

Their replacements were Warrington-based brewer Greenall Whitley, who were looking to extend into the north-east. Shirts appeared emblazoned with 'Greenall's Beers' and a lifting of the TV ban extended the coverage.

The following seasons saw the word 'Beers' dropped from the shirts, before the deal ended after a home draw with Swindon Town in December 1990.

Three days later came the return of Newcastle Breweries and a Blue Star logo on the home kits and black 'McEwan's Lager' lettering on the away shirt. Fans owning now-obsolete Greenalls replica shirts were offered free Blue Star patches to mask the old advertisers!

The next change came in the opening weeks of the 1993/94 season, when home shirts appeared with 'McEwan's Lager' lettering in gold. These gave way to a white on black version of the same design, alternating with the Blue Star – an arrangement continuing into the following season. 1995, though, saw the Blue Star design downsized and relegated to use only on the away kit.

The Newcastle Brown Ale bottle logo replaced it on the home shirts, proving an instant hit and selling in unprecedented quantities. This had an early pre-season airing at Hartlepool in July 1995. That classic logo then survived numerous shirt design changes before a farewell in May 2000 as the brewery sponsorship ended with a home win against Arsenal.

There was one oddity in this era, however. An on-air alcohol advertising ban on French TV led Newcastle to wear shirts advertising holiday park brand 'Centerparcs' for their European tie at Monaco (logo-free shirts had been worn earlier that season in Metz).

Season 2000/01 saw cable TV company NTL's logo appearing on shirts, as part of a deal by which they acquired a stake in the club.

Local building society Northern Rock then began an association with Newcastle that continues up until the present day, shirts first going on sale in May 2003. The Magpies wore the new kit for the first time in the pre-season Asia Cup tournament against Birmingham City in July of that year, with subsequent kit design changes incorporating the 'Northern Rock' legend in varying colours including blue, gold and white.

— TRANSFER TRAIL II —

In chronological order, the record transfer fees received for Newcastle players are:

Player	Year	Fee	Received from
Bobby Templeton	1904	£375	Woolwich Arsenal
Albert Shepherd	1914	£1,500	Bradford City
Hughie Gallacher	1930	£10,000	Chelsea
Albert Stubbins	1946	£12,500	Liverpool
Len Shackleton	1948	£20,050	Sunderland
Ernie Taylor	1951	£25,000	Blackpool
George Eastham	1960	£47,500	Arsenal
Alan Suddick	1966	£63,000	Blackpool
Bryan Robson	1971	£120,000	West Ham United
Terry McDermott	1974	£170,000	Liverpool
Malcolm Macdonald	1976	£333,333	Arsenal
Irving Nattrass	1979	£375,000	Middlesbrough
Peter Withe	1980	£500,000	Aston Villa
Chris Waddle	1985	£590,000	Tottenham Hotspur
Peter Beardsley	1987	£1,900,000	Liverpool
Paul Gascoigne	1988	£2,300,000	Tottenham Hotspur
Andy Cole	1995	£7,000,000	Manchester United
Deitmar Hamann	1999	£7,500,000	Liverpool
Jonathan Woodgate	2004	£13,667,000	Real Madrid

— ALL THE WAY FROM GUAM —

While far from the only former Magpie to manage internationally, Willie McFaul's stint in charge of Guam is undoubtedly the most exotic (although Peter Withe's time with Thailand and Indonesia and John Burridge's Oman posting had their moments).

Having ended his association with Newcastle when removed from the manager's job in 1988, McFaul had returned to his native Northern Ireland and was coaching Ballymena-based side Cullybackey Blues when he was approached by FIFA to help develop the round ball game on Guam, remote island in the western Pacific Ocean.

When he arrived in 1999, he discovered that the Guam FA (established by an Irish priest in 1975) had a few fundamental problems to overcome. An eight-team football league (including the fantastically-named Crushers) struggled for both fans and players, competing against the counter-attractions of baseball, basketball and American Football that were the staple sports on the military bases located on this US Dependency.

McFaul set about building a team, despite only having seven players at his first training session and losing more than one promising youngster to a college sports scholarship in the USA

A first foray into World Cup qualifying fixtures in November 2000, however, ended with his side making the headlines for the wrong reasons. Hampered by an arduous 48-hour journey to Iran to play in unfamiliar cold and wet conditions, McFaul's side (many of whom had never left Guam before) were thrashed 19–0 by Iran. They improved slightly two days later, going down 16–0 to Tajikistan.

Unbowed but struggling financially, Guam continued to play international football, competing in a qualifying tournament for the East Asian Cup in 2003, which required them to travel to Hong Kong.

Things started badly with an 11–0 loss to the hosts, followed by a 7–0 defeat to Chinese Taipei. However, although his side failed to score, McFaul took some satisfaction from successive 2–0 losses at the hands of Macao and Mongolia.

With the Japanese FA expressing an interest in developing the game on Guam and keen to bring in a coach with J-League experience, McFaul saw out his contract and departed in 2004, returning to a coaching position with the Northern Ireland FA.

— EARLY DOORS —

On Saturday January 18th 2003, Kevin Keegan's Manchester City side visited St James' Park with former Newcastle defenders Steve Howey and Sylvain Distin lining up for the visitors. Just before kick-off Alan Shearer was presented with the Goal of the Month award for a rapier strike against Everton the previous month – and was soon to be hogging the limelight again.

The match got underway with City defending the Leazes End and after kicking off, Howey played the ball back towards his goalkeeper Carlo Nash. Enter Shearer, who raced in and charged down Nash's attempted clearance before passing the ball into the unguarded net. The goal was timed at 10.4 seconds, with no other Newcastle player having touched the ball.

Newcastle went on to win the game 2–0, but Shearer's goal dominated the post-match coverage, being confirmed as the quickest strike of his career and the club's fastest-ever goal in top-flight football.

However, Jackie Milburn's effort in a Second Division game against Cardiff City on November 22nd 1947 is unofficially believed to be the fastest competitive goal for the club. No confirmed measure of the goal time exists, but the goalscorer himself later gave it as six seconds. The Magpies went on to win that match 4-1.

It was quickly established via TV replays that Shearer had just missed out on the record for the fastest ever Premiership goal. That accolade is held by Tottenham defender Ledley King, who netted in a fraction less than 10 seconds in a 3–3 draw against Bradford City at Valley Parade on December 9th 2000.

"I didn't think I had the legs to run half the length of the pitch in 10 seconds. I certainly couldn't have done it late in the game," said Shearer after the game.

— SUPERMAC'S QUICKFIRE GOAL —

Anecdotal evidence gives Malcolm Macdonald the record of scoring the fastest-ever goal in a public match involving the Newcastle first team. That happened at the start of a 7–3 pre-season friendly win over Scottish side St Johnstone on July 29th 1972.

Spotting Saints goalkeeper Derek Robertson still going through his warm-up routine, Macdonald took John Tudor's pass from the kick-off and netted from just inside the St Johnstone half – the goal unofficially timed at four seconds.

— CORNERS OF A FOREIGN FIELD —

Since Newcastle made their away bow in Rotterdam on a Tuesday night back in September 1969, up until the start of the 2007/08 season the club have played 60 away ties in various European competitions. In those games, the Magpies have played in 24 countries against 53 sides in 52 different stadia:

Season/competition	Opponent	Venue
1968/69 Fairs Cup	Feyenoord	De Kuip Stadion, Rotterdam
1968/69 Fairs Cup	Sporting Lisbon	Arvelade Stadium, Lisbon
1968/69 Fairs Cup	Real Zaragoza	Romareda Stadium, Zaragoza
1968/69 Fairs Cup	Vitoria Setubal	Arvelade Stadium, Lisbon
1968/69 Fairs Cup	Glasgow Rangers	Ibrox Park, Glasgow
1968/69 Fairs Cup	Ujpesti Dozsa	Megyeri uti Stadion, Budapest
1969/70 Fairs Cup	Dundee United	Tannadice Park, Dundee
1969/70 Fairs Cup	FC Porto	Estadio das Antas, Porto
1969/70 Fairs Cup	Southampton	The Dell, Southampton
1969/70 Fairs Cup	Anderlecht	Parc Astrid, Brussels
1970/71 Fairs Cup	Inter Milan	Giuseppe Meazza, Milan
1970/71 Fairs Cup	Pecsi Dozsa	Pecsi Vasutas Sport Kor, Pecs
1977/78 UEFA Cup	Bohemians	Dalymount Park, Dublin
1977/78 UEFA Cup	SEC Bastia	Stade Armand Cesari de Furiani
1994/95 UEFA Cup	Royal Antwerp	Bosuil Stadion, Antwerp
1994/95 UEFA Cup	Atletico Bilbao	San Mames, Bilbao
1996/97 UEFA Cup	Halmstads	Orjans vall Stadion, Halmstad
1996/97 UEFA Cup	Ferencvaros	Ulloi uti Stadion, Budapest
1996/97 UEFA Cup	AS Metz	Stade Saint-Symphorien, Metz
1996/97 UEFA Cup	AS Monaco	Stade Louis II, Monaco
1997/98 Champions League	Croatia Zagreb	Maksimir Stadium, Zagreb
1997/98 Champions League	Dynamo Kiev	Olympic Stadium, Kiev
1997/98 Champions League	PSV Eindhoven	Philips Stadium, Eindhoven
1997/98 Champions League	Barcelona	Nou Camp, Barcelona

1998/89 Cup Winner's Cup	Partizan Belgrade	JNA Stadium, Belgrade
1999/00 UEFA Cup	CSKA Sofia	Balgarska Armia, Sofia
1999/00 UEFA Cup	Zurich	Letzigrund, Zurich
1999/00 UEFA Cup	AS Roma	Olympic Stadium, Rome
2001/02 Intertoto Cup	Sporting Lokeren	Daknam Stadium, Lokeren
2001/02 Intertoto Cup	1860 Munich	Olympic Stadium, Munich
2001/02 Intertoto Cup	Troyes	Stade de l'Aube, Troyes
2002/03 Champions League	NK Zeljeznicar	Kosevo Stadium, Sarajevo
2002/03 Champions League	Dynamo Kiev	Olympic Stadium, Kiev
2002/03 Champions League	Juventus	Stadio Delle Alpi, Turin
2002/03 Champions League	Feyenoord	De Kuip Stadion, Rotterdam
2002/03 Champions League	Barcelona	Nou Camp, Barcelona
2002/03 Champions League	Bayer Leverkusen	BayArena, Leverkusen
2002/03 Champions League	Inter Milan	Giuseppe Meazza, Milan
2003/04 Champions League	Partizan Belgrade	JNA Stadium, Belgrade
2003/04 UEFA Cup	NAC Breda	MyCom Stadium, Breda
2003/04 UEFA Cup	FC Basel	St Jakob Park, Basel
2003/04 UEFA Cup	Valerenga IF	Ulleval Stadium, Oslo
2003/04 UEFA Cup	Real Mallorca	Estadi Son Moix, Palma
2003/04 UEFA Cup	PSV Eindhoven	Phillips Stadium, Eindhoven
2003/04 UEFA Cup	Olympique de Marseille	Stade Velodrome, Marseille
2004/05 UEFA Cup	Hapoel Bnei Sakhnin	Ramat Gan Stadium, Tel Aviv
2004/05 UEFA Cup	Panionios	Nea Smyrni Stadium, Athens
2004/05 UEFA Cup	Sochaux	Stade Auguste Bonal, Sochaux
2004/05 UEFA Cup	Heerenveen	Abe Lenstra Stadium, H'veen

2004/05 UEFA Cup	Olympiakos	Karaiskakis Stadium, Athens
2004/05 UEFA Cup	Sporting Lisbon	Arvelade Stadium, Lisbon
2005/06 Intertoto Cup	FK ZTS Dubnica	Mestsky Stadium, Dubnica
2005/06 Intertoto Cup	Deportivo La Coruna	Riazor Stadium, La Coruna
2006/07 Intertoto Cup	Lillestrom	Arasen Stadium, Oslo
2006/07 UEFA Cup	FK Ventspils	Skonto Stadium, Riga
2006/07 UEFA Cup	Levadia Tallinn	A. Le Coq Arena, Tallinn
2006/07 UEFA Cup	Palermo	Renzo Barbera, Palermo
2006/07 UEFA Cup	Eintracht Frankfurt	Commerzbank Arena, Frankfurt
2006/07 UEFA Cup	Zulte Waregem	Jules Otten Stadium, Ghent
2006/07 UEFA Cup	AZ Alkmaar	DSB Stadium, Alkmaar

— SEMI SUCCESS —

Newcastle have won 13 FA Cup semi-finals. Here is the full list of the club's semi-final triumphs:

Season	Score	Opponent	Venue
1904/05	1–0	Sheffield Wednesday	Hyde Road, Manchester
1905/06	2–0	Arsenal	Victoria Ground, Stoke
1907/08	6–0	Fulham	Anfield, Liverpool
1909/10	2–0	Swindon Town	White Hart Lane, London
1910/11	3–0	Chelsea	St.Andrews', Birmingham
1923/24	2–0	Manchester City	St.Andrews'
1931/32	2–1	Chelsea	Leeds Road, Huddersfield
1950/51	0–0	Wolverhampton Wanderers	Hillsborough, Sheffield
1950/51 (replay)	2–0	Wolverhampton Wanderers	Leeds Road
1951/52	2–1	Blackburn Rovers	Elland Road, Leeds
1954/55	1–1	York City	Hillsborough
1954/55 (replay)	2–0	York City	Roker Park, Sunderland
1973/74	2–0	Burnley	Hillsborough
1997/98	1–0	Sheffield United	Old Trafford, Manchester
1998/99	2–0	Tottenham Hotspur	Old Trafford, Manchester

— DOUBLE AGENTS —

"This for me is the derby to end all derbies. It can rival Glasgow and is more passionate than Manchester, Liverpool and certainly London. Other derbies have never generated such huge feeling, such elation and deep gloom."

Bobby Moncur (who played on both sides) summing up the mood that envelops the region when Newcastle United and Sunderland face each on the field.

As well as Moncur, other players to have appeared in senior football for both sides are:

William Agnew	Stan Anderson
John Auld	Harry Bedford
Paul Bracewell	Michael Bridges
Ivor Broadis	Alan Brown
Steve Caldwell	Johnny Campbell
Lee Clark	Jeff Clarke
Joe Devine	John Dowsey
Dave Elliott	Robbie Elliott
Ray Ellison	Alan Foggon
Howard Gayle	Tommy Gibb
Shay Given	Thomas Grey
Ron Guthrie	Tom Hall
Steve Hardwick	Mick Harford
John Harvey	David Kelly
Alan Kennedy	James Logan
Andy McCombie	Bob McDermid
Albert McInroy	Bob McKay
Bobby Moncur	James Raine
Ray Robinson	Bobby Robinson
Bryan Robson	Tom Rowlandson
Len Shackleton	Jock Smith
Colin Suggett	Ernie Taylor
Bob Thomson	Thomas Urwin
Barry Venison	Chris Waddle
Nigel Walker	Billy Whitehurst
Dave Willis	David Young

— MCC: MAGPIES CRICKET CLUB —

It's appropriate that a club which can trace their origins back to local cricket sides (see *From Eastenders to West End Boys*, page 1) should have signed a number of players who also showed some prowess with bat and ball.

Here's a Newcastle United XI made up of players who also shone in all white:

Player	On the books of
James Beaumont	Leicestershire
Kevin Brock	Wark (Northumberland League)
Ian Davies	Somerset
Harry Hardinge	Kent
Steve Harper	Easington (Durham Leagues)
Keith Kettleborough	Rotherham Town (Yorkshire League)
John Mitten	Leicestershire, Nottinghamshire, Lancashire
Peter Ramage	Tynemouth (North-East League)
Malcolm Scott	Northamptonshire
Arthur Turner	Hampshire
Sam Weaver	Derbyshire, Somerset

A willing 12th man for this imaginary side would be England pace bowler Steve Harmison, who cured his injury woes under the expert eyes of the Newcastle United medical staff. Magpies season ticket holder Harmison has gone on record as saying he'd willingly have given up cricket had he been given the opportunity to play professional football.

And the man nicknamed 'Toon Harmy' has appeared for the Magpies, lining up in 2005 alongside the likes of Robbie Elliott and Peter Ramage in a training ground friendly against the celebrity XI preparing for the Sky TV *The Match* series.

Barring an unexpected playing contract for Harmison though, the only player to have represented Newcastle United and played test match cricket remains Harry Hardinge – who did so some 13 years after leaving St James' Park.

The batsman widely known as 'Wally' in cricketing circles was selected for England in the Third Test against Australia in July 1921 at Headingley. Hardinge managed a knock of 25 in the first innings but fell after making just five in the second innings. The visiting side won by 219 runs, taking an unassailable 3–0 lead in the five-match series and thus retaining the Ashes.

— AD INFINITUM PART I —

A selection of TV advertisements that have featured former and future Newcastle United players and managers over the years:

Adidas (1996)
At the height of Newcastle's 'entertainers' fame, the iconic black and white home strip with Newcastle Brown Ale logo starred in a series of commercials for the shirt manufacturer. The adverts featured the likes of Kevin Keegan, Peter Beardsley and Les Ferdinand in various situations – including Keegan storming out of his office to remonstrate with Ferdinand, who is practicing his shooting by blazing the ball continually off the wall and disturbing 'the boss'. Prophetically, Keegan was prematurely aged for one shoot – appearing as a wrinkled, grey-haired old man relying on a walking stick. Some unkind media references to this were made when a drawn-looking KK resigned as Newcastle boss the following year . . .

Asda (2006)
Michael Owen joined the list of pocket-tappers in time for the World Cup.

Barclaycard (2001)
Sir Bobby Robson was shown buying rollerskates on his plastic.

Barclays (2004)
Some computer-based trickery in this commercial devised by agency Bartle Bogle Hegarty saw Sir Bobby Robson travelling to a Newcastle home game by bus, only to then encounter himself in a bewildering variety of guises.Bobbys young and old, big and small could be seen – there was even one wearing a dress. Other Premiership managers also featured in the ad, including current Newcastle boss Sam Allardyce, while a miniature Sir Alex Ferguson was screened getting a piggyback at one point. The campaign ended at the time of Robson's dismissal from the Toon hotseat.

Brut (1970s)
Kevin Keegan advertised "the great smell of Brut" aftershave in cahoots with ex-boxer Henry Cooper, who famously urged men to "splash it all over".

BT (1998)
Newcastle boss Kenny Dalglish was filmed at home making a series of phone calls and saying things like "thanks for your support" and "best you've been all season". Asked by his daughter Kelly why he'd changed his habit of not ringing players after games, Kenny replied, "I'm ringing

up the crowd" and, "only another 34,000 to go!" In a fantastically ill-timed airing, the advert was first screened on the weekend that Dalgish's Newcastle side were soundly beaten 4–1 at Leeds.

Carlsberg (2006)
An ad with the strapline, "Probably the best pub team in the world" saw Sir Bobby Robson managing an old England side featuring Jack Charlton, Stuart Pearce, Peter Beardsley and Chris Waddle in a Sunday morning kickabout.

Domino's Pizza (2006)
Owen again, this time in a plot which involved being locked in a cupboard. No wonder he injured himself in Germany.

Lancia Cars (1989)
During Ruud Gullit's time at AC Milan, he starred in this Italian-only advert, in which he leaves training in such a hurry that he drives off across the pitch. The groundsman was not available for comment.

L'Oreal Shampoo (1998)
"Because I'm worth it," emoted David Ginola in his seductive Gallic tones. His contract included a stipulation that he didn't cut his hair short.

Lucozade (1994)
Starred future Magpie John Barnes rambling on about isotonic drinks and hoofing a can in a bin. Michael Owen and Alan Shearer also appeared in ads for the drink.

— ON THE ROAD AGAIN —

When Newcastle United made their competitive debut at Reading's Madejski Stadium on April 30th 2007 it was the 46th different ground that the Toon have appeared at in the Premiership – playing 39 different sides in the process.

Of these 39, they have played eight teams at two different grounds. They are:

Opponent	Stadia
Arsenal	Highbury, Emirates Stadium
Bolton Wanders	Burnden Park, Reebok Stadium
Derby County	Baseball Ground, Pride Park
Fulham	Craven Cottage, Loftus Road
Leicester City	Filbert Street, Walkers Stadium
Manchester City	Maine Road, City of Manchester Stadium
Southampton	The Dell, St. Mary's Stadium
Sunderland	Roker Park, The Stadium of Light

— NICKNAMES PART I —

A selection of nicknames from the earlier years of Newcastle United's history:

'Daddler'	Andy Aitken
'Cockles	Bill Appleyard
'Knocker'	Thomas Bartlett
'Ankles'	Albert Bennett
'Rock of Tyneside'	Frank Brennan
'Big Sandy'	Alex Caie
'Hughie'	Joe Ford
'Punky'	Alex Gardner
'The Duke	Doug Graham
'Wally'	Harry Hardinge
'Diddler'	Albert Harris
'Tiger'	Jimmy Hill
'Hurricane Hutch'	Duncan Hutchison
'Camel'	Vic Keeble
'The Laughing Cavalier'	Wilf Low
'Bobby Dazzler'	Bobby Mitchell
'Tucker'	Tom Mordue
'Scots Wullie'	Bill McPhillips
'Peter the Great'	Peter McWilliam
'Clown Prince of Soccer'	Len Shackleton
'Tadger'	Jimmy Stewart
'The Silent Assassin'	Albert Stubbins
'Topper'	Tommy Thompson
'Ginger'	Jack Wilkinson
'Monte'	Johnny Wilkinson

— IT'S WOR CUP . . . SOMETIMES —

Of 354 FA Cup ties played by Newcastle up to the start of the 2007/08 season, United have won 175, drawn 82 and lost 97.

The club's biggest FA Cup victory remains a 9–0 success against Southport in season 1931/32 – this coming after two 1–1 draws in the first two matches of the tie, resulting in this second replay being staged at the neutral venue of Hillsborough, Sheffield.

A 1–7 reverse at Villa Park against Aston Villa in season 1896/97 is Newcastle's heaviest defeat in the competition. Villa went on to complete a League and FA Cup Double.

To date, the Magpies have netted 647 times and conceded 434 goals in the FA Cup (not including penalty shoot-outs).

— NEWCASTLE LEGENDS: TONY GREEN —

Tony Green: Still revered on Tyneside

"It was the saddest day of my life: he was my very best buy. I could watch him play all day and every day." The words of then Newcastle boss Joe Harvey provide some insight into why Tony Green was worshipped by the St James' Park faithful during his brief spell with Newcastle before injury forced his retirement at the age of just 26.

A fantastic combination of speed on the ball, close control and balance had made Green the idol of Bloomfield Road after he joined Blackpool from Albion Rovers in his native Glasgow. Alerted to his promise and goalscoring prowess alongside former Magpie Alan Suddick in the Blackpool midfield, Don Revie tried to sign Green for Leeds United after he had proved his fitness again following a year-long lay-off through injury.

However, Revie found himself out of the loop when the old boy network smoothed the passage of Green's transfer to St James' – Harvey and Blackpool boss Bob Stokoe were former Newcastle team-mates in the 1950s.

For Harvey, Green's arrival on Tyneside in October 1971 relieved the pressure on a side who had slipped to second from bottom in the league. Green took some of the midfield burden from Terry Hibbitt, helping to provide an improvement in the service to striker Malcolm Macdonald and a subsequent climb up the table.

Blackpool, meanwhile, received £90,000 in cash plus striker Keith Dyson, who Stokoe hoped would boost his side's efforts at achieving promotion from Division Two.

Green become an instant terrace hero in his first season at Newcastle and he collected numerous man of the match awards despite the club's unexceptional eleventh place finish and infamous FA Cup exit at Hereford United.

Of his 27 league appearances that season, the victory at Old Trafford one week after the nightmare on Edgar Street remains one of his most celebrated displays. Although Green didn't score that day, his domination of the midfield was lauded in the press and hopes were high that the following season would see the club challenge for major honours once more.

In the event Harvey's side improved their Division One finishing position by three spots, finishing eighth. However, that was to be achieved largely without the contribution of Green. On September 2nd 1972 he was stretchered off the field at Selhurst Park with a knee injury after a tackle by Crystal Palace hardman Mel Blyth.

Green endured three operations before an abortive comeback in a reserve game at Coventry in November 1973 confirmed the inevitable.

Middlesbrough provided the opposition for a testimonial in May 1974 – almost 30,000 supporters turning out despite having seen Newcastle beaten at Wembley less than a week earlier.

Moving back to the Lancashire coast, Green became a school teacher and served on the Pools Panel. His occasional visits to St James' Park still result in a rousing reception from supporters who remember his brief, but wonderful time in Toon.

Tony Green factfile
Born: Glasgow, October 13th 1946
Newcastle career: 38 apps, 3 goals (1971–73)
Other clubs: Albion Rovers, Blackpool
International: Scotland, 6 caps, 0 goals

— NEWCASTLE'S TOP 10 FA CUP SCORERS —

Player	Total
Jackie Milburn	23
Alan Shearer	21
Bobby Mitchell	18
Bill Appleyard	16
Albert Shepherd	16
Neil Harris	14
James Howie	14
Malcolm Macdonald	14
John Rutherford	14
Tom McDonald	13

— FRENCH FOREIGN LEGION —

Aside from Englishmen, Newcastle have relied on more French-born players during their 14 Premiership seasons than from any other nation – no fewer than 13 in all:

Player	Signed	From
David Ginola	July 1995	Paris St Germain
Stephane Guivarc'h	June 1998	Auxerre
Laurent Charvet	July 1998	Cannes
Didier Domi	November 1998	Paris St Germain
Louis Saha	January 1999	Metz (loan)
Alain Goma	June 1999	Paris St Germain
Franck Dumas	July 1999	Monaco
Olivier Bernard	September 2000	Olympique Lyonnais
Laurent Robert	August 2001	Paris St.Germain
Sylvain Distin	September 2001	Paris St.Germain (loan)
Charles N'Zogbia	July 2004	Le Havre
Jean-Alain Boumsong	January 2005	Glasgow Rangers
Antoine Sibierski	August 2006	Manchester City

The Magpies also signed three further French-born players who failed to make a competitive first-team appearance for the club:

David Terrier	January 1998	Unattached
Lionel Perez	June 1998	Sunderland
Olivier Bernard	September 2006	Unattached

Bernard was a free agent when he joined Newcastle for a second time in September 2006, his signing outside the transfer window being permissible after he was released from his playing contract with Glasgow Rangers.

— CAR TOON ARMY —

Driving misadventures involving Newcastle United players include:

September 1990 Five youth team players were injured when their car crashed and rolled over on the A1 in Durham. Driver Michael English and team-mates Phil Mason, Alan Thompson, John Watson and Michael Young were returning after seeing the reserves play at Leeds. Most severely injured was Thompson, who endured two operations on his damaged neck and spent nine months in a brace. He recovered however to enjoy the most successful career of the quintet, culminating in an England cap in 2004.

August 1998 Stuart Pearce walked away almost unscathed from an accident in Nottinghamshire, after his Rover 200 ended up being squashed by a council dustcart.

Pearce commented, "I know just how lucky I am to be alive."

May 1999 Driving his Porsche Boxster, Andy Griffin collided with a Metro train at Callerton Parkway. The Metro won. Then-manager Ruud Gullit said: "I don't know how you can drive into a train. I really don't know, but he's okay. We were more concerned about the Porsche!"

February 2000 Another accident involving youth team players, this time on the A189 to the north of Newcastle.

Kevin Wealleans plus team-mates Ryan Hogg, Johnny Mann and Paul Dunn all suffered injuries. Driver Wealleans spent time in intensive care.

April 2001 Driving his Mercedes, Nolberto Solano was stopped by police in Gosforth. He was banned and fined for drink-driving.

April 2001 Kieron Dyer was banned and fined after being caught speeding in his Mercedes near Durham. Magistrates heard he was listening to radio coverage of golfer Tiger Woods winning the US Open and he wasn't aware of his speed. Dyer later commented: "What can I say? I'm a huge Tiger Woods fan."

In the same month, Dyer sustained minor injuries after his Mercedes S320 collided with another car outside the club's training ground at Chester-le-Street.

December 2002 Kieron Dyer was fined after being convicted of speeding near Grantham in his BMW. In the same month, Dyer wrote off his Ferrari 360 Modena after it collided with the Swing Bridge over the River Tyne. He was unhurt but his passenger suffered whiplash.

December 2002 Dressed as Captain Hook, Clarence Acuna was returning from the players' fancy dress party when his Mercedes was stopped near Newcastle's Pilgrim Street police station. He was fined and banned for drink-driving.

May 2003 Serial offender Dyer was banned and fined after being caught speeding on the A167 in Durham.

June 2003 Nikos Dabizas smashed his car into traffic lights in Athens hours after playing for Greece. He scrambled free before his vehicle caught fire.

September 2005 Lee Bowyer was banned and fined after being caught speeding on the A1 in Northumberland.

August 2006 Driving his BMW, Titus Bramble hit a wall in the Norfolk village of Newton Flotman.

November 2006 Albert Luque stopped his Porsche Cayenne to check a puncture en route to Newcastle Airport, only for a skip lorry to plough into the back of it. He was unhurt.

— ENGLAND'S DREAMING —

Thirty-three players have appeared in the full England side while being on Newcastle United's books:

Player	Date	Opponent
Matt Kingsley	March 18th 1901	Wales (h)
Jackie Rutherford	April 9th 1904	Scotland (a)
Jack Carr	February 25th 1905	Ireland (h)
Albert Gosnell	February 17th 1906	Ireland (a)
Colin Veitch	February 17th 1906	Ireland (a)
Albert Shepherd	February 11th 1911	Ireland (h)
Jimmy Stewart	April 1st 1911	Scotland (h)
Charlie Spencer	April 12th 1924	Scotland (h)
Frank Hudspeth	October 24th 1925	Northern Ireland (a)
Tom Urwin	March 1st 1926	Wales (h)
Jack Hill	May 9th 1929	France (a)
Samuel Weaver	April 9th 1932	Scotland (h)
Jimmy Richardson	May 13th 1933	Italy (a)
Dave Fairhurst	December 6th 1933	France (h)
Duggie Wright	November 9th 1938	Norway (h)
Jackie Milburn	October 9th 1948	Northern Ireland (a)
Ivor Broadis	April 3rd 1954	Scotland (a)
Malcolm Macdonald	May 20th 1972	Wales (a)
Chris Waddle	March 26th 1985	Republic of Ireland (h)
Peter Beardsley	January 29th 1986	Egypt (a)

Rob Lee	October 12th 1994	Romania (h)
Steve Howey	November 16th 1994	Nigeria (h)
Barry Venison	September 7th 1994	USA (h)
Warren Barton	June 8th 1995	Sweden (h)
Les Ferdinand	December 12th 1995	Portugal (h)
Alan Shearer	September 1st 1996	Moldova (a)
David Batty	September 1st 1996	Moldova (a)
Kieron Dyer	September 4th 1999	Luxembourg (h)
Jermaine Jenas	February 12th 2003	Australia (h)
Jonathan Woodgate	March 31st 2004	Sweden (a)
Nicky Butt	August 18th 2004	Ukraine (h)
Michael Owen	September 7th 2005	Northern Ireland (a)
Scott Parker	October 11th 2006	Croatia (a)

Note: the dates and opponents given are the first appearance as a Magpie and therefore not necessarily the player's actual England debut.

Of these players, six marked that first appearance by scoring: Albert Shepherd, Jimmy Stewart, Jackie Milburn, Ivor Broadis, Rob Lee and Alan Shearer.

Meanwhile, Matt Kingsley, Duggie Wright and Nicky Butt all enjoyed the comfort of their England debut as a Newcastle player being staged at St James' Park.

Not included in the list is Paul Gascoigne, who made his England debut while a Tottenham Hotspur player in September 1988 – having moved from Newcastle just two months previously.

— BUY OR SELL ANY SPARES —

The first all-ticket FA Cup final was the 1924 meeting between Newcastle United and Aston Villa – the decision being taken following the chaos of the 'White Horse Final' between Bolton and West Ham 12 months previously when thousands of fans spilled onto the pitch delaying the start.

— NICKNAMES PART II —

Yet more Magpie monikers:

'The Bear'	Roy Aitken
'Prince'	Philippe Albert
'Dick'	David Barton
'Centre Parting'	Warren Barton
'Pedro'	Peter Beardsley
'Lurch'	Dave Beasant
'Bez'	John Beresford
'Bomber'	Ray Blackhall
'Scoop'	John Blackley
'Gnasher'	Lee Clark
'Seamus'	John Cowan
'The Mighty Wyn'	Wyn Davies
'Sir Les'	Les Ferdinand
'Sparrowhawk'	Diego Gavilan
'Sarge'	Paul Goddard
'Boy'	Steve Howey
'Ned'	David Kelly
'Killer'	Brian Kilcline
'Supermac'	Malcolm Macdonald
'Cassius'	Ron McGarry
'Psycho'	Stuart Pearce
'The Mighty Quinn'	Mick Quinn
'Rambo'	George Reilly
'Pop'	Bryan Robson
'Scoot'	Scott Sellars
'Jinky'	Jimmy Smith
'Cannonball'	Colin Taylor
'Bones'	Kenny Wharton

— BOARD GAMES —

Installed at a cost of £66,000 and paid for by Scottish and Newcastle Breweries, St James' Park's first electronic scoreboard made its debut on December 20th 1980 – hardly being tested by a dull 0–0 draw with Bristol City.

The new stadium feature replaced the previous manually operated cricket-type scoreboard, which displayed half-time scores at other grounds alongside a letter corresponding to listings in the match programme.

However, the new technology allowed for all sorts of 'extras', ranging from a fan-friendly time countdown and announcement of the attendance to rather less practical displays of 'winking eyes' and what looked like an assortment of badly-formed dancing Mister Men.

Sited behind the centre section of the uncovered Gallowgate End, an early design defect was noted by those fans who from time to time chose to climb onto it. The game score display relied on the name of the opponents being added for each game in temporary letters. Unfortunately these proved to be less than robust – leading to unfamiliar opponents such as 'elsea' appearing at St James' Park. Some other hitherto unknown teams also appeared on the half-time score lists – including 'Derby City' more than once.

An updated scoreboard was installed in 1988 with assistance from NEI, remaining in place until ground redevelopment reached that end in the close season of 1993.

The dot matrix type display of this scoreboard lent itself to more fanciful output, including some barely recognisable facial portraits of Newcastle players. Strangely, a large number of these belonged to players who barely featured for the club (eg John Robertson), while the Mick Quinn image was surely scanned from a photo of so-called TV entertainer Bob Carolgees.

At other times random messages would flash across the scoreboard with only the vaguest connection to on-pitch events – Jim Smith's side being routinely welcomed with 'the Eagle has landed', while sub-standard loan signing Dave Mitchell's only goal for the club was greeted by 'that's the magic of Mitchell'.

For the punters in the crowd, occasional 'big race' results were displayed – once with disastrous consequences. The 1989 Grand National was staged on Saturday April 8th, which coincided with Newcastle hosting Aston Villa. An on-screen announcement duly confirmed the winning horse as 'Liverpool Bear'.

Cue widespread grumbling and the disposing of apparently-worthless betting slips – with nobody seeming to have backed this hitherto unheard-of outsider (a real dark horse?) Unfortunately, it later came to light that a communication breakdown had resulted in the scoreboard operator mishearing the name of the actual winning horse, 'Little Polveir'.

The question of reinstalling a smaller scoreboard has often cropped up in recent years – with the stadium redevelopment ruling out the jumbo efforts seen elsewhere.

However, to date there have been no developments in this area.

— ALL THERE IN BLACK AND WHITE PART I —

A selection of vintage Magpie-related headlines from the written press:

'NORTH TRIUMPHS'
A slightly patronising *Daily Mirror* headline on the Monday following Newcastle United's 2–1 FA Cup Final success over Arsenal in April 1932.

'MILBURN A J.E.T'
The *Sunday Pictorial* created a suitable headline for their reporting of Newcastle United's 2–0 1951 FA Cup Final victory over Blackpool from the initials of the scorer's name.

'IT'S OURS'
Accompanying a report of the cup win, telephoned direct from the Empire Stadium by Stan Bell and published in the *Evening Chronicle*, 1951.

'IT'S OURS AGAIN!'
The obvious accompaniment to news of the 1952 Wembley trophy success. However, the *Evening Chronicle* actually kept this one under wraps until the 3–1 final victory over Manchester City in 1955 (the 1952 headline was "United Bring Home the Cup Again").

'HUGHIE OF THE MAGIC FEET IS DEAD'
The *Newcastle Journal* headline in June 1957, following the discovery of the body of former Magpie legend Hughie Gallacher, who had taken his own life by standing in front of a train.

'HARVEY BRAVES RIP TO EUROPE GLORY'
Confirmation of Newcastle United's Fairs Cup success in 1969 in the *Daily Mirror*.

'SALUTE SUPERMAC'
Tyneside's new hero celebrates his home debut with a hat-trick over Liverpool in August 1971, reports the *Daily Mirror*.

'GORDON WHO?'
The *Newcastle Evening Chronicle* back page headline that greeted new manager Gordon Lee in June 1975. The quote came from United striker Malcolm Macdonald, who was in South Africa when Tyneside journalist John Gibson broke the news to him.

— NOT SO SAFE HANDS —

Outfield players who have gone between the posts for Newcastle include:

Player	Year	Fixture	Comp	Score
John King	1915	Tottenham Hotspur (a)	League	0-0
John Nesbitt	1958	Petrolul Ploesti (a)	Friendly	2–3
Chris Waddle	1983	Leeds United (a)	League	1–0
Chris Hedworth	1986	West Ham United (a)	League	5–8
Peter Beardsley	1986	West Ham United (a)	League	1–8
Kevin Brock	1992	Birmingham City (a)	League	3–2

The Hedworth/Beardsley appearances took place in one amazing night at the Boleyn Ground in April 1986. Newcastle had taken to the field with a clearly unfit Martin Thomas between the posts and reserve keeper Dave McKellar sidelined with a hip injury.

After Thomas had further damaged his injured shoulder and conceded four goals, he was replaced by Ian Stewart at the interval with 22-year-old defender Chris Hedworth going in goal on what was only his tenth (and final) appearance for the club.

Hedworth was then also injured whilst challenging Tony Cottee as the West Ham striker scored the fifth goal and also had to be withdrawn, reducing the Magpies to ten men.

Peter Beardsley then took over goalkeeping duties and won the applause of the crowd with some good stops, but ultimately conceded three goals – and left his manager, former Newcastle keeper Willie McFaul calling this the most bizarre game of his career.

West Ham defender Alvin Martin scored a remarkable hat-trick in this game – netting once past each of the three 'keepers. Meanwhile, future Newcastle and West Ham manager Glenn Roeder didn't help the visitors' cause by scoring an own goal.

— IT'S ALL BALLS —

The first time that Newcastle supporters – or at least those with access to a wireless – were able to hear the FA Cup draw 'live' was when the BBC broadcast the third round draw on 16th December 1935.

On that occasion, the Magpies were handed a trip to the Anlaby Road ground of Hull City – a tie that they won 5–1.

It is recorded that the FA Secretary Stanley Rous was requested that day "to ensure that the bag is shaken for a few seconds to produce a distinctive and suitable sound".

— CAN WE PLAY YOU EVERY WEEK? —

Since Premiership football arrived at St James' Park in August 1993, the most welcome (and benevolent) visitors in terms of points gained have been Everton. Here's the complete record of Newcastle's Premiership points earned, and from whom, at St James'Park:

Opposition	Frequency	Record	Points
Everton	14 visits	9 wins, 3 draws, 2 defeats	30
Aston Villa	14 visits	9 wins, 2 draws, 3 defeats	29
Southampton	12 visits	9 wins, 1 draw, 2 defeats	28
Tottenham Hotspur	14 visits	8 wins, 3 draws, 3 defeats	27
Chelsea	14 visits	7 wins, 4 draws, 3 defeats	25
Coventry City	8 visits	7 wins, 1 draw, 0 defeats	22
Liverpool	14 visits	6 wins, 4 draws, 4 defeats	22
Middlesbrough	11 visits	6 wins, 4 draws, 1 defeat	22
West Ham United	12 visits	6 wins, 4 draws, 2 defeats	22
Arsenal	14 visits	5 wins, 5 draws, 4 defeats	20
Blackburn Rovers	12 visits	5 wins, 4 draws, 3 defeats	19
Bolton Wanderers	8 visits	6 wins, 1 draw, 1 defeat	19
Leicester City	8 visits	6 wins, 1 draw, 1 defeat	19
Manchester City	9 visits	6 wins, 1 draw, 2 defeats	19
Leeds United	11 visits	5 wins, 3 draws, 3 defeats	18
Sheffield Wednesday	7 visits	5 wins, 1 draw, 1 defeat	16
Derby County	6 visits	5 wins, 1 draw, 0 defeats	16
Wimbledon	7 visits	5 wins, 1 draw, 1 defeat	16
Charlton Athletic	8 visits	3 wins, 4 draws, 1 defeat	13
Manchester United	14 visits	3 wins, 4 draws, 7 defeats	13
Nottingham Forest	4 visits	4 wins, 0 draws, 0 defeats	12
Portsmouth	4 visits	3 wins, 1 draw, 0 defeats	10
Birmingham City	4 visits	3 wins, 0 draws, 1 defeat	9
West Bromwich Albion	3 visits	3 wins, 0 draws, 0 defeats	9
Fulham	6 visits	2 wins, 2 draws, 2 defeats	8
Ipswich Town	4 visits	2 wins, 2 draws, 0 defeats	8
Sunderland	6 visits	2 wins, 2 draws, 2 defeats	8
Norwich City	3 visits	2 wins, 1 draw, 0 defeats	7
Queens Park Rangers	3 visits	2 wins, 0 draws, 1 defeat	6
Watford	2 visits	2 wins, 0 draws, 0 defeats	6
Wigan Athletic	2 visits	2 wins, 0 draws, 0 defeats	6
Crystal Palace	3 visits	1 win, 1 draw, 1 defeat	4
Barnsley	1 visit	1 win, 0 draws, 0 defeats	3
Oldham Athletic	1 visit	1 win, 0 draws, 0 defeats	3
Reading	1 visit	1 win, 0 draws, 0 defeats	3

Sheffield United	2 visits	1 win, 0 draws, 1 defeat	3
Swindon Town	1 visit	1 win, 0 draws, 0 defeats	3
Bradford City	2 visits	0 wins, 1 draw, 1 defeat	1
Wolverhampton Wanderers	1 visit	0 wins, 1 draw, 0 defeats	1

— ALL ABOARD THE SKY LARK —

To coincide with their 1,000th live transmission of a Premiership fixture in May 2007, Sky TV asked presenter Richard Keys to compile a top ten of memorable games.

Despite having never won the competition, Newcastle United still figured prominently in the list, featuring in half the games selected:

Southampton 2 Newcastle United 1 (October 24th 1993)
Blue strips for Newcastle, but red faces after two pieces of brilliance from Matthew Le Tissier. More Dell Hell followed, with a touchline fall-out between Kevin Keegan and Lee Clark.

Newcastle United 0 Manchester United 1 (March 4th 1996)
Peter Schmeichel in the Gallowgate goal was battered constantly for 45 minutes but held firm. Eric Cantona scored the vital goal and changed the destiny of the title.

Liverpool 4 Newcastle United 3 (April 3rd 1996)
Routinely trotted out as the best Premiership encounter ever televised – although the corresponding fixture twelve months later with the same scoreline ran it close . . .

Leeds United 0 Newcastle United 1 (April 29th 1996)
The post-match utterances of Kevin Keegan (see *Mind Games*, page 86) make this memorable.

Newcastle United 5 Manchester United 0 (October 20th 1996)
Sheer brilliance. Immortalised in the video release *Howay 5–0*.

— MIND GAMES —

April 29th 1996. Newcastle have just won 1–0 at Elland Road against Leeds United and Kevin Keegan is interviewed live on Sky Sports:

Kevin Keegan: "I think you've got to send Alex Ferguson a tape of this game, haven't you? Isn't that what he asked for?"

Andy Gray (Sky pundit): "Well I'm sure if he was watching it tonight, Kevin, he could have no arguments about the way Leeds went about their job and really tested your team."

Kevin Keegan: "And . . . and . . . we . . . we're playing Notts Forest on Thursday and . . . he objected to that! Now that was fixed up four months ago. We f . . . supposed to play Notts Forest. I mean that sort of stuff, we . . . is it's been . . . we're bet, we're bigger than that."

Richard Keys (Sky Anchorman): "But that's part and parcel of the psychology of the game, Kevin, isn't it?"

Andy Gray: "No, I don't think so."

Kevin Keegan: "No! When you do that, with footballers, like he said about Leeds. And when you do things like that about a man like Stuart Pearce . . . I've kept really quiet, but I'll tell you something, he went down in my estimation when he said that.

"But I'll tell ya – you can tell him now if you're watching it – we're still fighting for this title and he's got to go to Middlesbrough and get something, and I tell you honestly, I will l love it if we beat them . . . love it!"

Richard Keys: "Well, quite plainly the message is, it's a long way from over and you're still in there scrapping and battling and you'll take any of these just as long as you continue to get the results?"

Kevin Keegan: "I think football in this country is so honest and so . . . honestly, when you look sometimes abroad, you've got your doubts. But it really has got to me and I, I, I've not voiced it live, not in front of the press or anywhere – I'm not even going to the Press Conference. But the battle's still on and Man United have not won this yet!"

While the 'love it' segment is routinely used to illustrate Keegan's misplacement of the plot, the full text tells a different story.

Keegan's reference to Pearce stemmed from Newcastle agreeing to participate in the Nottingham Forest defender's testimonial – eight days after the two sides were due to meet in a Premier League fixture.

Alex Ferguson then publicly claimed Forest would go easy on Newcastle because of Pearce's influence and that Leeds would similarly slacken off against Keegan due to their hatred of the Red Devils.

In the event Newcastle's title bid crumbled in a 1–1 draw at Forest, while the one team which lied down and died proved to be former

United star Bryan Robson's Middlesbrough – allowing Manchester United the freedom of the Riverside on the final day of the season, the Red Devils claiming the title after a 3–0 victory on Teesside.

— THE FINAL COUNTDOWN, OR NOT? —

Opinion remains divided over whether the everyday phrase 'back to square one' can be attributed to the first live radio commentaries of sporting events – including one featuring Newcastle United.

The development of portable broadcasting equipment persuaded the BBC to venture into sports events, with a successful experiment to transmit live radio commentary from the England versus Wales rugby union fixture at Twickenham in January 1927. To coincide with this event, the BBC published a diagram of the playing surface divided into eight equal, numbered sections in that week's *Radio Times*. Then as the commentator broadcast news of the play, a second voice solemnly intoned the square number where the action was taking place.

Judged a success, the enterprise decamped to Highbury the following week, where coverage of the Arsenal versus Sheffield United fixture was broadcast, with a similar grid again being published.

Seven days later the BBC broke further new ground by transmitting their first-ever FA Cup tie. The game chosen was the fourth round match between First Division leaders Newcastle United and the renowned amateur side Corinthians – who had only compromised on their principles of non-competitiveness in order to participate in the FA Cup for the first time in 1922.

With the BBC's commentator Captain Henry Blythe Thornhill 'Teddy' Wakelam at the microphone, wireless set owners (with their *Radio Times* grids at the ready) and 56,338 supporters at the Crystal Palace ground in Sydenham heard and saw United end their winless run at this venue with a 3–1 success.

It has long been claimed that the act of the ball moving into the first square on the grid.in other words right back to one end of the pitch, gave rise to the popular phrase 'back to square one'. However, doubt was cast on the tale by the BBC themselves, in an edition of the TV programme *Balderdash and Piffle* in 2006. This questioned the fact that the phrase was in general use before World War II, disputing whether the actual phrase was ever uttered as part of the grid commentary.

— BLACK AND WHITE AND READ ALL OVER —

Saturday December 17th 2005 saw the final curtain fall on a Tyneside sporting institution, when the final edition of the *Pink* rolled off the printing presses at Thomson House.

A dedicated sports newspaper that had been produced by the *Evening Chronicle* for 110 years under various titles, with an (almost) kick-by-kick report of Newcastle's game that afternoon painstakingly rung in from the ground and recorded by copytakers.

Along with results (and later scorers) from the rest of the Football League and that all-important pools information, the whole thing was somehow bundled together, printed and distributed across the region by early evening.

The advent of mobile phone technology and text messaging however ultimately saw sales drop to an unacceptable level. The mortal blow though was the growth of Sky TV – bringing scores instantly into pubs and homes, while also ending the tradition of Saturday afternoon games.

Various attempts to provide alternative content in the *Pink* were made, but ultimately Newcastle's dominance of Sunday live schedules was to provide decisive. Gimmicks like making the publication date Saturday and Sunday just didn't work.

While the coverage of grassroots football, rugby and other minority sports such as speedway attracted some devotees, too few readers were prepared to fork out the increasing cover price on a non-match day, even if Sunderland had lost.

Prior to the 1963/64 season the paper was produced on normal newsprint, but a 3–1 home victory over Derby County on August 24th 1963 was the subject matter of the first 'Sports Edition' to be printed on the distinctive pink paper (although the title didn't change for a number of years).

At least the last-ever edition was able to report on a significant success – that of a 4–2 victory at West Ham for Newcastle, featuring a Michael Owen hat-trick.

The *Pink* name lives on in cyberspace, with post-match reports appearing under that banner on the icnewcastle website.

Some classic *Pink* headlines:

Aug 1971	'Mac Cracks In Super Three'	Newcastle United 3
		Liverpool 2
Aug 1982*	'Kev's Big Day a Hit'	Newcastle United 1
		QPR 0

Jan 1990	'Cloud Nine'	Newcastle United 5 Leicester City 4
Feb 1992**	'It's A Kracker'	Newcastle United 3 Bristol City 0
May 1992	'Safe!'	Leicester City 1 Newcastle United 2
Apr 1999	'Four-midable'	Derby County 3 Newcastle United 4
Feb 2000	'Red and Buried'	Newcastle United 3 Manchester Utd 0
Sep 2002	'Toons of Glory'	Newcastle United 2 Sunderland 0
Apr 2005+	'Disgrace'	Newcastle United 0 Aston Villa 3
Dec 2005	'Owe Yes!'	West Ham United 2 Newcastle United 4

* Kevin Keegan's playing debut for the club.
** Kevin Keegan's managerial debut for the club.
+ Lee Bowyer and Kieron Dyer sent off for fighting with each other.

— TOON TALISMEN —

Newcastle United's top ten Premiership goalscorers:

Player	Total
Alan Shearer	148
Peter Beardsley	47
Andy Cole	43
Les Ferdinand	41
Nolberto Solano	37
Robert Lee	34
Gary Speed	29
Shola Ameobi	27
Craig Bellamy	27
Kieron Dyer	23
Laurent Robert	22

— THE HIGH NUMBERS —

Having missed out on the debut Premiership football season, Newcastle United began their so-far unbroken 14-season stint in the competition allocating squad numbers to players for the first time in preparation for the 1993/94 season.

Saturday August 14th 1993 saw Kevin Keegan's side at home to Tottenham Hotspur and the squad for that game was announced as:

1	Pavel Srnicek	12	Mark Robinson
2	Barry Venison	13	Tommy Wright
3	John Beresford	14	Alex Mathie
4	Paul Bracewell	15	Brian Kilcline
5	Kevin Scott	16	Liam O'Brien
6	Steve Howey	17	Nicky Papavasiliou
7	Robert Lee	18	Kevin Brock
8	Peter Beardsley	19	Steve Watson
9	Andy Cole	20	Alan Neilson
10	Lee Clark	21	Unallocated
11	Scott Sellars	22	Richie Appleby

By the time a fixture with Arsenal ended that first season, that list had seen the following additions and amendments:

5	Ruel Fox	26	Robbie Elliott
13	Unallocated	27	Unallocated
16	Unallocated	28	Unallocated
21	Malcolm Allen	29	Brian Reid
23	Chris Holland	30	Mike Hooper
24	Matty Appleby	31	Mike Jeffry
25	Unallocated		

Subsequent seasons have seen numerous alterations, the highest number allocated and used to date being the 45 that Hugo Viana donned in 2002.

The most high-profile transfer of a number came in 1996 when Les Ferdinand was persuaded to vacate the number 9 shirt for a certain £15 million signing. It is claimed that Ferdinand was then refused permission by the Premier League to wear the 99 shirt, although in his autobiography the player wrote that he requested 23 in honour of basketball star Michael Jordan. But after the club demanded that he choose a number in the first XI, Ferdinand eventually ended up with 10, Lee Clark being press-ganged into moving to 20.

— TWO-TIME TOONS —

Players who enjoyed two separate spells on the books of Newcastle United include:

Player	First Spell	Second Spell
Peter Beardsley	1983–87	1993–97
John Burridge	1989–91	1993
Lee Clark	1989–97	2005–06
John Craggs	1964–71	1982–83
Bobby Cummings	1954–56	1963–65
Robbie Elliott	1991–97	2001–06
Robert Gibson	1911–12	1919–20
Mick Harford	1980–81	1982
Terry Hibbitt	1971–75	1978–81
George Luke	1950	1959–61
Terry McDermott	1973–74	1982–84
Mark McGhee	1977–79	1989–91
David Mills	1982	1983–84
George Nevin	1925	1928–30
Ken Prior	1952–54	1956–57
Jimmy Richardson	1928–34	1937–38
Pavel Srnicek	1991–98	2006–07
Tommy Wright	1988–93	1999

The shortest return was undoubtedly that of striker Mick Harford, who rejoined Newcastle on a free transfer from Bristol City after the Ashton Gate side defaulted on their payments, before immediately being sold on to Birmingham City.

A number of other players have subsequently returned to serve at St James' Park in an off-field capacity, including managerial trio Joe Harvey, Kevin Keegan and Glenn Roeder.

Inside-right Charlie Woods can claim the longest gap between stints at Newcastle. Transferred from Newcastle to Bournemouth and Boscombe Athletic in 1962, Woods returned as part of Sir Bobby Robson's backroom team in 2000 – a period of just under 38 years.

— BOER BORE —

Of particular note among Newcastle's many pre and post-season tours was the 1952 jaunt to Southern Africa, when the FA Cup holders were accompanied by the trophy, thanks to a special licence being granted for it to be taken out of Great Britain.

In total, the tour took 70 days to complete, with the party travelling over 21,000 miles in the process. No fewer than 16 friendly matches were played, with Newcastle scoring 73 goals in the process.

Newcastle travelled with 16 players: Ron Batty, Frank Brennan, Bobby Cowell, Charlie Crowe, Reg Davies, Bill Foulkes, George Hannah, Joe Harvey, Jackie Milburn, Bobby Mitchell, Alf McMichael, Ted Robledo, George Robledo, Ronnie Simpson, Bob Stokoe and Tommy Walker.

Both George Robledo and Jackie Milburn picked up injuries in the early games which restricted their involvement (Milburn played just five times) and forced trainer Norman Smith to play defender Frank Brennan in an unfamiliar forward role.

The best individual scoring performance came in the Border Province fixture, when George Robledo weighed in with seven of the ten goals scored.

When questioned by reporters when the party eventually arrived back in England, captain Joe Harvey was scathing in his criticism of the tour itinerary, saying: "The unending travelling, the hard grounds and the atmospheric conditions were ordeals and I, for one, am glad it's all over. We should have played fewer games and we should have made Johannesburg the base instead of being hawked around South Africa non-stop."

Date	Opposition	Result
17th May	Southern Transvaal	won 3–2
21st May	Natal	won 6–2
24th May	Natal	won 4–0
31st May	Western Province	won 8–0
4th June	Griqualand West	won 3–0
7th June	Northern Transvaal	won 2–1
10th June	Lourenco Marques	won 5–0
14th June	Northern Rhodesia	won 6–1
18th June	Southern Rhodesia	won 4–2
21st June	East Transvaal	won 2–0
25th June	Orange Free State	won 3–0
28th June	South Africa	won 3–0 (in Durban)
2nd July	Border Province	won 10–0
5th July	Eastern Province	won 5–1
12th July	South Africa	lost 3–5 (in Johannesburg)
16th July	Southern Transvaal	won 6–4

— #9 DREAM PART II —

As well as the appearance ex-Toon striker Albert Stubbins on the cover of the *Sgt. Pepper* . . . album by the Beatles (see *#9 Dream Part I*, page 35) a second Magpies/Fab Four-related piece of artwork hit the shelves of the world's record shops during the 1970s.

On October 4th 1974 John Lennon's new album *Walls and Bridges* was released on the Apple/EMI label. While the music isn't remembered as vintage Lennon material despite the presence of guests such as Elton John, the cover artwork captured the work of Lennon the artist. The centrepiece of an intricate fold-out sleeve designed by Roy Kohara is a colour painting entitled 'Football' along with the legend 'John Lennon June 1952 age 11'.

That date and the clear depiction of players wearing the red and white of Arsenal and the black and white of Newcastle United confirm the subject of the painting to be a scene from 1952 FA Cup Final – which the Magpies won 1–0 at Wembley in May of that year.

And while the quality of the drawing is no better than the average 11-year-old would produce, it seems certain that the moment captured is the scoring of the only goal of the game, which came six minutes from full time.

In Lennon's picture, scorer George Robledo is seen tussling with Gunner's defender Lionel Smith in the air, with the ball just about to pass goalkeeper George Swindin en route to the Arsenal net. The whole scene is watched by a fourth player, Newcastle's number nine Jackie Milburn.

However, a November 2005 reissue of *Walls and Bridges* substituted this artwork for a photograph of Lennon taken by Bob Gruen.

— JOSSY'S GIANTS —

Written by TV darts commentator and fanatical Toon fan Sid Waddell, the TV show *Jossy's Giants* recounted the story of Jossy Blair, who after seeing his promising career as a Newcastle United player wrecked by injury, opened a sports shop ('Magpie Sports') and started coaching a junior football team.

Inevitably, the script called for a trip to St James' Park in an episode called 'The Promised Land' and Jossy and co. duly rolled up, to be met by Bobby Charlton and then-Magpies boss Willie McFaul, who guided them round the ground and onto the hallowed turf.

— NEWCASTLE LEGENDS: JOE HARVEY —

Joe Harvey: Honorary Geordie

Had Stan Seymour not been accorded the nickname 'Mister Newcastle', then Joe Harvey would have laid strong claim to it – like Seymour he served the club for many years as both captain and manager. As it is though, Harvey is one of a number of former Magpies deserving of the title of honorary Geordie – settling on Tyneside in preference to his native Yorkshire.

Spotted playing for Bradford City during World War II (when he scored twice against Newcastle), Harvey moved to St James' Park for £4,250 in October 1945.

He made his competitive debut for the club in 1946, in the same FA Cup tie against Barnsley as Jackie Milburn. Appointed captain, Harvey led by example on the field and had no problem making himself heard, having previously served as Company Sergeant-Major in the Royal Artillery.

A mainstay of the Newcastle side at right-half from 1946 to 1953 and a double FA Cup winner, Harvey then moved into the backroom staff before parting company with the club after the 1955 FA Cup Final to begin his managerial career.

He spent two years at Barrow, then moved the short distance to Workington,where he signed striker Ron McGarry, who was to follow Harvey when he returned to Tyneside as Newcastle manager in 1962.

Taking over a recently-relegated side which had flirted with a second relegation, Harvey rebuilt the team with new signings and graduates from the 1962 FA Youth Cup-winning side, eventually achieving promotion back to the First Division at the third attempt in 1964/65.

The summit of his footballing achievements came four years later when Newcastle brought European silverware back to Tyneside in 1969 – the second leg of the Inter-Cities Fairs Cup Final coinciding with Harvey's 51st birthday.

Having enjoyed Wembley success twice with the club on the field, defeat in the 1974 FA Cup Final against Liverpool proved to be a bitter blow and one from which Harvey never fully recovered, leaving his post within a year after some fans turned on him.

He remained on the staff at Gallowgate though, returning in a caretaker manager capacity in 1980 at the age of 62, while the club sought to appoint a replacement after sacking Bill McGarry.

Harvey died in February 1989, aged 70. His funeral, unlike Jackie Milburn's the previous year, was a low-key affair but nonetheless he remains firmly in the affections of generations of Newcastle supporters.

Joe Harvey factfile
Born: Edlington, November 6th 1918
Died: February 24th 1989
Newcastle career: 247 apps, 12 goals
Other clubs: Wolverhampton Wanderers, Bournemouth, Bradford

— THE FOREIGN LEGION —

Players born outside the British Isles to have played first team football for Newcastle:

Player	Year signed	Country of birth
George Robledo	1949	Chile
Ted Robledo	1949	Chile
Arnold Woollard	1952	Bermuda
Preben Arentoft	1969	Denmark
Andy Parkinson	1978	South Africa
Frans Koenen	1980	Netherlands
Tony Cunningham	1985	Jamaica
Mirandinha	1987	Brazil
Bjorn Kristensen	1989	Denmark
Frank Pingel	1989	Denmark
Alan Neilson	1989	Germany
Pavel Srnicek	1990, 2006	Czech Republic
Nicky Papavasiliou	1993	Cyprus
Marc Hottiger	1994	Switzerland
Philippe Albert	1994	Belgium
David Ginola	1995	France
Faustino Asprilla	1996	Colombia
Jimmy Crawford	1997	USA
Alessandro Pistone	1997	Italy
Temuri Ketsbaia	1997	Georgia
Jon Dahl Tomasson	1997	Denmark
John Barnes	1997	Jamaica
Andreas Andersson	1998	Sweden
Nicos Dabizas	1998	Greece
Laurent Charvet	1998	France
Dietmar Hamann	1998	Germany
Nolberto Solano	1998, 2005	Peru
Stephane Guivarc'h	1998	France
George Georgiadis	1998	Greece
Didier Domi	1999	France
Louis Saha	1999	France
Silvio Maric	1999	Croatia
Marcelino	1999	Spain
Alain Goma	1999	France
Franck Dumas	1999	France
John Karelse	1999	Netherlands
Fumaca	1999	Brazil

Helder	1999	Angola
Diego Gavilan	2000	Paraguay
Daniel Cordone	2000	Argentina
Shola Ameobi	2000	Nigeria
Lomana Tresor Lua Lua	2000	DR Congo
Clarence Acuna	2000	Chile
Christian Bassedas	2000	Argentina
Olivier Bernard	2000, 2006	France
Laurent Robert	2001	Reunion Islands
Sylvain Distin	2001	France
Hugo Viana	2002	Portugal
Patrick Kluivert	2004	Netherlands
Charles N'Zogbia	2004	France
Ronny Johnsen	2004	Norway
Celestine Babayaro	2005	Nigeria
Jean-Alain Boumsong	2005	Cameroon
Amdy Faye	2005	Senegal
Emre	2005	Turkey
Albert Luque	2005	Spain
Craig Moore	2005	Australia
Matty Pattison	2006	South Africa
Obafemi Martins	2006	Nigeria
Giuseppe Rossi	2006	Italy
Antoine Sibierski	2006	France
David Edgar	2006	Canada
Oguchi Oneywu	2007	USA

— KEEPING UP APPEARANCES —

Newcastle United's top ten Premiership appearance-makers:

Player	Total
Shay Given	313
Alan Shearer	303 (including 8 as substitute)
Robert Lee	267 (including 11 as substitute)
Nolberto Solano	229 (including 19 as substitute)
Gary Speed	213 (including 7 as substitute)
Aaron Hughes	205 (including 12 as substitute)
Kieron Dyer	190 (including 21 as substitute)
Warren Barton	162 (including 21 as substitute)
Shola Ameobi	162 (including 69 as substitute)
John Beresford	136 (including 3 as substitute)

— CHAIRMEN OF THE BOARD —

The men who have held the power at St James' Park:

Chairman	Appointed
Alex Turnbull	1892
D McPherson	1893
John Cameron	1894
Alex Turnbull	1895
William Nesham	1895
James Telford	1901
John Cameron	1904
Joseph Bell	1908
James Lunn	1909
George T Milne	1911
George G Archibald	1913
John Graham	1915
John P Oliver	1919
David Crawford	1928
James Lunn	1929
George F Rutherford	1941
John W Lee	1949
Robert Rutherford	1951
Stan Seymour	1953
Wilf Taylor	1955
William McKeag	1958
Wallace E Hurford	1959
William Westwood	1964
Robert J Rutherford	1978
Stan Seymour Junior	1981
Gordon McKeag	1988
George Forbes	1990
Sir John Hall	1991
Freddy Shepherd	1996
Sir John Hall	1998
Freddy Shepherd	1998

— NEWCASTLE LEGENDS: BOBBY MONCUR —

Bobby Moncur: Desperate to lose the title
'last Newcastle captain to lift a major trophy'

No major cup tie featuring Newcastle would be complete without Bobby Moncur pleading for the current wearer of the armband to unseat him from his position as the last captain to lift a trophy for the club.

Since that balmy night in Budapest in 1969 when Moncur accepted the Fairs Cup from Sir Stanley Rous, no Toon skipper has come close to lifting further silverware.

The son of a policeman (who played centre half for the force), Perth-born Moncur came to the attention of Newcastle in 1960 as a 15-year-old playing for Scotland schoolboys. After summer trials that year with Preston North End, Wolverhampton Wanderers and Manchester United, Moncur turned down them all to sign for Newcastle.

Initially an inside-left, Moncur scored four times against West

Wylam when guesting for the junior side and signed amateur forms before agreeing to put pen to paper as an apprentice for Charlie Mitten's squad in October 1960.

After rising through the junior and reserve sides and captaining the former to FA Youth Cup success in 1962, Moncur signed a full professional contract and made his debut as an 18-year-old away to Luton Town in March 1963.

By then he was playing under Joe Harvey and had moved back into defence with some success, covering for injuries in the reserve side earlier that year. However, Moncur was to only feature sporadically for the first team, filling in at various times across the field. Such was his frustration at failing to gain a regular spot in the side that he asked to move on in 1967. Norwich City and Brighton and Hove Albion showed interest, but a move to the Canaries stalled when they were unwilling to meet Newcastle's £25,000 asking price.

After Newcastle's inconsistent start to the 1967/68 season, Moncur won a place in defence and impressed so much that he remained an ever-present, took the captain's armband from Frank Clark and ended the season with his first full Scotland cap.

The following season he enhanced his reputation by leading Newcastle to Fairs Cup glory – although few could have predicted that his first three senior goals for the club would all come in the two-legged final against Hungary's Ujpesti Dozsa.

Moncur's final game in a black and white shirt came at Wembley against Liverpool in the 1974 FA Cup Final, before he left St James' Park for a two-year stint at Sunderland.

Coaching and management jobs at Carlisle United (where he signed a young Peter Beardsley), Heart of Midlothian, Plymouth Argyle, Whitley Bay and Hartlepool United followed, before he ceased to be actively involved in the game in 1989.

Since then Moncur has been involved in various different recreational activities including managing a squash centre, working at a golf club and skippering ocean-going yachts – both competitively and in the leisure market.

He has also continued to watch Newcastle United as an on-air pundit for local radio.

Bobby Moncur factfile
Born: Perth, January 19th 1945
Newcastle career: 361 apps, 10 goals
Other clubs: Sunderland, Carlisle United
International: Scotland, 16 apps, 0 goals

— FULL HOUSE —

Since Newcastle United were promoted to the Premiership, no outfield player has completed an ever-present season of league appearances. However goalkeeper Shay Given has achieved that record on no fewer than four occasions, spending every minute of all 38 games between the posts in seasons 2001/02, 2002/03, 2003/04 and 2005/06.

The last outfield player who started every league game in a season was Lee Clark, with the midfielder wearing the number 10 shirt for all 46 Division One fixtures in 1992/93. Unfortunately, his replacement by substitute Gavin Peacock in the second half of the home game against Notts County denied the Tynesider a perfect record that season.

Midfielder Gary Speed was involved in every Premiership game of both the 1998/99 and 2003/04 seasons, but that record included four substitute run-outs in the former and one in the latter.

Another occupant of the number 10 shirt had a similar record in season 1989/90, striker Mark McGhee starting all 46 Division Two games. For good measure, the Scot was also in the starting XI for the two play-off games and the seven cup ties Newcastle played that season. McGhee's replacement by substitute Paul Sweeney in a home game against Oxford United cost him a full house though.

You have to go back to season 1985/86 for the last example of an outfield player appearing in every minute of every game for the Magpies. That was defender Glenn Roeder, who completed all 42 Division One games and was also on the field for the duration of the club's four cup games that season – one of which included extra-time. Not far behind him that same season was Peter Beardsley, who also made 42 league starts but was substituted once and also missed one of the cup ties.

In terms of the number of games in a season, the record set by Bryan 'Pop' Robson back in 1968/69 remains intact to this day. The striker was an ever-present in every minute of the Magpies' 42 Division One fixtures and also all the club's cup games – this being Newcastle's legendary Fairs Cup-winning season. Beginning the season with a goal in a 1–1 home draw with West Ham in August 1968, 'Pop' was still going strong in Budapest against Ujpesti Dozsa the following June when the trophy was claimed – a total of 59 appearances.

— TEENAGE KICKS PART I —

Since taking their bow in the inaugural season of 1952/53, Newcastle United have captured the FA Youth Cup twice.

Season 1961/62 began with a resounding 14–0 success over Seaton Delaval, before amateur side Corinthians were defeated 3–0 on Tyneside. A 3–1 victory at Roker Park then led to a fourth round tie at Old Trafford against Manchester United – who had won the competition in the first five years it was staged. Goals from future first team players Bobby Moncur and Alan Suddick helped the young Magpies to a 2–1 victory. It's notable that at the time Moncur was playing as a forward, having been unable to force his way into the defence.

A repeat of that scoreline then overcame local side North Shields and set up a two-legged semi-final against Portsmouth. The Magpies travelled to Hampshire by train and during the journey goalkeeper Stan Craig contrived to accidentally smash a carriage window and sit in the broken glass. He was able to play after having three stitches inserted in his backside, but couldn't stop Pompey from taking a one goal lead into the second leg.

A wet evening on Tyneside though saw United concede a further goal to trail by two at the interval. Some hope came from a Les O'Neil effort on 58 minutes, but with Pompey scoring again soon after, a first final appearance was only secured after a supreme effort. Goals from Matty Gowland, Les O'Neil again and a fine chip from George Watkin though won the day and set up a two-legged final against Wolverhampton Wanderers.

Nearly 14,000 fans were at Molineux to see the sides draw 1–1, Clive Chapman equalising for United with a memorable individual goal in which he dribbled past three opponents. The return leg on Tyneside saw 20,588 in attendance at Gallowgate, with the vital goal coming when Bobby Moncur headed home a Les O'Neil corner at the near post.

A week later, Moncur signed his first professional contract with Newcastle United. The club were also billed £10 for the damage to the train window. Eight of the final side went on to feature in the Magpies first team: David Craig, Colin Clish, John Markie, Bobby Moncur, Les O'Neil, Alan Suddick, Dave Turner and George Watkin. The other three players were: Clive Chapman, Stan Craig and Matty Gowland. Alan Wilkinson played in earlier rounds before being injured.

— LEAGUE CUP FINAL ONE-OFF —

Newcastle's sole League Cup final appearance came in February 1976, when Manchester City won 2–1 at Wembley thanks to goals from Peter Barnes and an acrobatic bicycle kick from Geordie Dennis Tueart. Alan Gowling had equalised for Newcastle.

The cup run began with a second round tie against Division Four side Southport that was switched from Haig Avenue to St James' Park in order to earn the Lancashire club extra revenue.

Bristol Rovers of Division Four were then beaten after a draw at Eastville and a replay on Tyneside, before Division One side QPR were overcome at Loftus Road for the second successive season in this competition.

A quarter-final tie with Second Division Notts County followed and despite Newcastle enjoying home advantage, the other Magpies proved to be tricky opponents until goalkeeper Eric McManus fumbled a long Macdonald throw into his own net.

A trip to Wembley was then secured after the team turned round a one-goal deficit from the first leg at White Hart Lane in a memorable home display against Tottenham Hotspur.

Manchester City, meanwhile, had overcome Norwich City, Nottingham Forest, Manchester United and Mansfield Town, and a Tyne-Tees final was avoided when Tony Book's side disposed of Jack Charlton's Middlesbrough at the semi-final stage.

The road to Wembley:

Round	Opponent	Score	Scorers
Second	Southport (h)	6–0	Gowling 4, Cannell 2
Third	Bristol Rovers (a)	1–1	Gowling
Third Replay	Bristol Rovers (h)	2–0	T. Craig (pen), Nattrass
Fourth	Queens Park Rangers (a)	3–1	Macdonald, Burns, Nulty
Fifth	Notts County (h)	1–0	McManus (og)
Semi-final (1)	Tottenham Hotspur (a)	0–1	
Semi-final (2)	Tottenham Hotspur (h)	3–1	Gowling, Keeley, Nulty
Final	Manchester City (n)	1–2	Gowling

— INTERNATIONALISTS —

Newcastle United fielded a starting XI composed entirely of full internationals for the first time in their history when Everton visited St James' Park on February 28th 1998:

Player	Country
Shay Given	Republic of Ireland
Warren Barton	England
Steve Howey	England
Stuart Pearce	England
Philippe Albert	Belgium
David Batty	England
Robert Lee	England
Gary Speed	Wales
Alan Shearer	England
Andreas Andersson	Sweden
Keith Gillespie	Northern Ireland

However, despite putting out this stellar line-up and even bringing on a substitute with full international experience (Georgia's Temuri Ketsbaia), Kenny Dalglish's side were held to a 0–0 draw.

— BACK TO THE FUTURE —

Future Newcastle players and managers who picked up FA Youth Cup honours earlier in their careers, include:

Year	Player	Playing for
1953	Albert Scanlon	Manchester United
1954	Albert Scanlon	Manchester United
1967	Colin Suggett	Sunderland
1970	Graeme Souness	Tottenham Hotspur
1970	Ray Clarke	Tottenham Hotspur
1973	Dave McKellar	Ipswich Town
1977	Kenny Sansom	Crystal Palace
1978	Kenny Sansom	Crystal Palace
1989	Jason Drysdale	Watford
1992	Nicky Butt	Manchester United
1993	Keith Gillespie	Manchester United
1996	Michael Owen	Liverpool
1997	Jonathan Woodgate	Leeds United

— NEUTRAL TERRITORY —

As well as being used as a venue for international matches over the years, St James' Park has hosted various competitive club fixtures not featuring Newcastle United:

Date	Result	Competition
April 18th 1903	Sunderland 2 Middlesbrough 1	Division One
December 23rd 1935	Hartlepool 4 Halifax Town 1	FA Cup replay
February 6th 1952	Gateshead 0 West Bromwich A 2	FA Cup replay
March 13th 1954	Bishop Auckland 5 Brigg Sports 1	FA Amateur Cup
April 19th 1954	Bishop Auckland 2 Crook Town 2	FA Amateur Cup
November 28th 1955	Carlisle United 1 Darlington 3	FA Cup replay
March 17th 1956	Bishop Auckland 5 Kingstonian 1	FA Amateur Cup
March 16th 1957	Bishop Auckland 2 Hayes 0	FA Amateur Cup
March 12th 1960	Crook Town 1 Kingstonian 2	FA Amateur Cup
March 28th 1964	Crook Town 2 Barnet 1	FA Amateur Cup
January 16th 1967	Middlesbrough 4 York City 1	FA Cup replay
March 18th 1972	Blyth Spartans 0 Enfield 0	FA Amateur Cup
February 27th 1978	Blyth Spartans 1 Wrexham 2	FA Cup replay
September 3rd 1994	Gateshead 0 Yeovil Town 3	GM Vauxhall Conference

The Wear-Tees derby of April 1903 was played on Tyneside as a punishment for Sunderland, after their fans had stoned the motor coach carrying players of The Wednesday (later Sheffield Wednesday) on Wearside earlier that month.

The only other occasion when the stadium has been used for a league match not involving Newcastle came in 1994, when cross-Tyne neighbours Gateshead were unable to play at their usual home venue due to an athletics meeting taking place at the International Stadium.

United allowed their fellow Tynesiders use of St James' Park, giving Yeovil fans among the 2,734 crowd their first – and so far only – opportunity to see the Glovers play at Gallowgate.

The appearance of the visitors was fitting, given that Newcastle had provided the opposition four years previously when Yeovil christened their new Huish Park ground.

— CAUGHT IN THE TRIANGLE —

Thanks to some underachievement in the FA Cup in January 1986, fourth round day arrived with Newcastle lacking a fixture. A 0–2 home reverse at the hands of Brighton had ended the Magpies' Wembley dreams for another year, while Brian Clough's Nottingham Forest were similarly underemployed – having lost to Blackburn Rovers in a replay.

A friendly match between the two stages was duly arranged – but in the slightly unexpected and thoroughly exotic venue of Bermuda.

Thanks to a sponsorship deal brokered with a Nottingham-based businessman, the two sides were flown out to the tropical island and faced each other at the Somerset Cricket Club ground in Sandys Parish.

The final score was a resounding 0–3 defeat at the hands of Forest, whose goals came from David Campbell (2) and Ian Bowyer.

Just over a fortnight later the two sides met again, this time in a Division One fixture. On that occasion, two Peter Beardsley goals gave Willie McFaul's side ample revenge at the City Ground – in rather chillier conditions.

That completed a hectic period for Beardsley, who had taken part in the Bermuda game before flying on to Egypt, linking up with the England squad and making his full international debut in Cairo.

— CELEBRITY FANS PART II —

A further selection of celebrity supporters often associated with the club:

Sting
The Wallsend-born former bus conductor, labourer and tax officer, real name Gordon Sumner, who became lead singer of 'The Police' and multi-million album-selling solo star. Doubts do persist, however, over his previous alleged mackem affiliations.

Jimmy Nail
The actor/singer otherwise known as James Michael Aloysius Bradford is reputed to have missed a schoolboy trial with the Magpies because he didn't manage to get out of bed. A trial of a different kind then saw him imprisoned later in life – convicted following an outbreak of violence after a Newcastle away game. His TV appearances have often included references to the club, especially in *Auf Wiedersehen Pet* and *Spender* – a detective series set on Tyneside which used St James' Park as a backdrop for an episode entitled 'The Golden Striker'. Nail is related to Newcastle player (and 1924 FA Cup winner) Edward Mooney.

Sid Waddell
Best known as an enthusiastic TV darts commentator, Sid watched his hero Bobby Mitchell from the terraces as a youngster and later managed to name check Mitch when penning the children's TV series *Jossy's Giants*.

Norman Wisdom
Despite being a childhood Arsenal fan and former director of Brighton and Hove Albion, the veteran actor and comedian has had a black and white allegiance since a meeting with a Geordie squaddie during World War II.

Wisdom has made the journey to Tyneside from his home in the Isle of Man on numerous occasions over the years. He was a guest of honour when England faced Albania at St James' Park in a World Cup Qualifier in September 2001. Some familiar larking about on the field before kick-off delighted the visiting Albanians – for whom Wisdom remains a national hero (he was one of very few foreign actors whose films were broadcast by the state TV station during years of communist rule).

— A QUESTION OF VEXILLOLOGY —

Some flag-related stories:

- Reports of a riot that took place before the scheduled Tyne-Wear derby match of April 1901 mention that the club flag was torn down by rampaging Sunderland fans. Images of St James' Park at that time show a flag flying from the south-west corner of the stadium, but by the 1950s a large Union Jack flag can be seen fluttering from a flag pole at the South East corner.
- The same location also saw the so-called 'ten-minute flag' fly for some years – a large flag with black and white vertical stripes displayed throughout the match until taken down to indicate that the 80th minute had been reached.
- The club's revival in the 1990s then saw Newcastle supporters club together and buy a large flag. This was unfurled for the first time in April 1992 from the East Stand, after victory over Sunderland virtually secured promotion. The horizontally-striped black and white flag read:

NEWCASTLE UNITED
TOON ARMY
CHAMPIONS 1992/93

This flag became a familiar sight at games, being passed back and forward over the heads of fans. It made a belated comeback at Watford's Vicarage Road in the final game of the 2006/07 season.

- An even bigger flag then appeared in the 1993/94 season: another horizontal black and white effort emblazoned with a brewery blue star, two Magpie cartoon figures and the legend:

NEWCASTLE UNITED
HOWAY THE LADS

This was also displayed within St James' Park but later labelled a fire risk and banned.

After being draped from the partially-built Gallowgate Stand when Arsenal were beaten in May 1994, the flag then followed the club into Europe. Numerous appearances on the continent followed, including matches at Antwerp and Metz. However this second flag met its end during the November 1997 trip to Barcelona – failing to make it back from the rain-sodden Nou Camp.

- A third large flag did briefly appear in the 2004/05 season, complete with club badge. This was funded by Newcastle United and unfurled before the FA Cup semi-final tie with Manchester United at Cardiff's Millennium Stadium in April 2005. It also made a brief appearance at St James' Park before a home game.
- Alan Shearer's retirement in May 2006 was marked by a large banner showing him in familiar goalscoring celebration style and titled 'Thanks for Ten Great Years'. This was draped from the back of the Gallowgate Stand in the days leading up to his testimonial against Celtic.
- Another Shearer-related creation made the headlines in April 1998, when a giant replica 'Shearer 9' shirt briefly adorned the 'Angel of the North' sculpture. The mission to clothe Anthony Gormley's statue on the southern approaches to Tyneside was carried out by a group of supporters in the run up to the Wembley FA Cup final involving Newcastle and Arsenal. Fishing lines and catapults were used to hoist the 29 feet by 17 feet replica strip into place early one morning, although it was quickly lowered once the police became aware.

— TRIPLE CROWN —

The last time Newcastle competed in a League game for two points was on May 2nd 1981, when the Toon beat Orient 3–1 at St James' Park to complete an unmemorable eleventh-place finish in Division Two.

The following season three points were up for grabs for the first time when Watford were the opening day visitors to Tyneside. However, Newcastle went down 0–1 to the Hornets and were beaten 0–3 at Loftus Road by Queens Park Rangers the following week. It was only at the third attempt that a three point maximum was recorded, thanks to a 1–0 win over Cambridge United at St James' Park on September 12th 1981. The all-important goal came from midfielder John Trewick.

— NEWCASTLE LEGENDS: JIMMY LAWRENCE —

*Jimmy Lawrence: A geat keeper, although the balls
were a lot bigger in those days!*

The statistics speak for themselves – record appearance maker,
three First Division championship winners' medals, one FA Cup
winner's medal and an unbroken 18-year spell on the books at
Gallowgate.

Glaswegian keeper Jimmy Lawrence was signed by Newcastle in

July 1904, taking the place of Charlie Watts between the posts in a 2–0 home win over Manchester City in October of that year.

A first championship medal followed that season, but so too did the first of four FA Cup Final defeats – two of which (in 1908 and 1911) came as a direct result of costly individual errors on Lawrence's part.

However, he was to pick up a winner's medal in 1910 against Barnsley – the first of two consecutive seasons when he appeared in FA Cup finals and replays.

Further championship-winning seasons followed in 1906/07 and 1908/09 – the latter being one of three seasons when Lawrence was an ever-present in both league and cup. And during his long Newcastle career, Lawrence boasted the enviable record of having saved four of the five penalty kicks he faced against Sunderland in Tyne-Wear derby fixtures.

Surprisingly for such a consistent performer he was only capped by Scotland once, in a Home International game against England in 1911 at Everton's Goodison Park.

Lawrence played his final game for Newcastle in April 1922 at home to Bradford City, before giving way to his successor Bill Bradley and moving on shortly after to become manager of Division Two side South Shields. A spell in charge of Preston North End followed, before he was persuaded to join German side Karlsruhe.

He enjoyed title success with the club in 1925, before returning to his native Scotland where he served Stranraer as both a director and chairman up until his death in 1934.

Jimmy Lawrence factfile

Born: Glasgow, February 16th 1885   Died: November 1934

Newcastle career: 496 apps (1904–21)

Other clubs: Patrick Athletic, Hibernian, Newcastle United, South Shields (manager), Preston North End(manager), Karlsruhe (trainer), Stranraer (director and chairman).

International: Scotland, 1 cap

— SAFE HANDS . . . SOMETIMES —

Since their promotion from the old Division One in 1993, Newcastle have entrusted goalkeeping duties in their 540 Premiership games to just seven players:

Player	Year(s) played	Total	Subs
Shay Given	1997/present	313	0
Pavel Srnicek	1993/1998, 2006/2007	97	2
Shaka Hislop	1995/1998	53	0
Steve Harper	1994/present	46	5
Mike Hooper	1993/1996	23	2
Tommy Wright	1993,1999	5	1
Jon Karelse	1993/2003	3	0

Meanwhile, another six goalkeepers have taken their place on the substitutes' bench for the Magpies in the Premiership without being called into action:

John Burridge	1993
Tony Caig	2003/2006
Fraser Forster	2006/present
Peter Keen	1998/1999
Tim Krul	2006/present
Lionel Perez	1998/2000

Both Perez and Burridge played against Newcastle in the Premiership – for Sunderland and Manchester City respectively. Burridge kept a clean sheet in a 0–0 draw at Maine Road in April 1995 after appearing as a half-time replacement for Tony Coton. And as well as frustrating his former employers, who had released him six months earlier, that game saw him become the oldest player to appear in the Premiership, aged 43 years, four months and 26 days.

— ALL THERE IN BLACK AND WHITE PART II —

A selection of more recent Magpie-related headlines from the written press:

'KING KEVIN'

A suitable *Evening Chronicle* front page headline to accompany a photo of the Newcastle United manager Kevin Keegan wearing a crown, seconds after his side clinched promotion by winning at Grimsby Town in May 1993.

'HOT COLE'
Goal number 39 of the season for Magpies striker Andy Cole equalled the club's scoring record and helped United to a 2–0 victory over Liverpool at Anfield in 1994. *The Mirror* gauged the temperature nicely.

'HOWAY FIVE-0'
Surfing on a wave of mass hysteria on Tyneside, *The Sun* conjured up a classic headline to accompany their report of Newcastle United's 5–0 home success over Manchester United in October 1996.

'HO HO SEVEN'
It may have come three days after Christmas Day 1996, but Newcastle United's 7–1 home win over Tottenham Hotspur still prompted a seasonal effort from the *Sunday Mirror*.

'TEARS OF A TOON'
How *The Sun* reported reaction to the resignation of Kevin Keegan from the manager's job at Newcastle United, in January 1997.

'DREAM TEAM'
An epic night of European football on Tyneside in September 1997 ended with Barcelona on the wrong end of a Tino Asprilla treble.

'CLARKIE IN THE SHIRT'
News reached the *Sunday Sun* in June 1999 that then-Sunderland midfielder Lee Clark had been spotted at Wembley a month previously watching Newcastle United in the FA Cup Final. His attire for part of that day? A T-shirt with the slogan 'sad mackem b*stards'.

'SHEARER THRIVES WITH FIVE'
The *Guardian* documented the return to goalscoring form of striker Alan Shearer in September 1999, as Bobby Robson oversaw his first home game in charge at St James' Park. Final score: Newcastle United 8 Sheffield Wednesday 0 (Shearer 5).

'WOR MIKEY'
How the *Daily Mirror* announced the arrival of Michael Owen to Tyneside in August 2005.

'FINAL'
The *Evening Chronicle* reporting on the career-ending injury suffered by Alan Shearer during Newcastle's 4–1 victory on Wearside in April 2006.

— MEET THE MANAGERS —

The complete list of the men in charge of the Newcastle United team through the years:

Manager	Years in charge
Frank Watt	1895–1930 (secretary)
Andy Cunningham	1930–1935
Tom Mather	1935–1939
Stan Seymour	1939–1947 (honorary)
George Martin	1947–1950
Stan Seymour	1950–1954 (honorary)
Duggie Livingstone	1954–1956
Charlie Mitten	1958–1961
Norman Smith	1961–1962
Joe Harvey	1962–1975
Gordon Lee	1975–1977
Willie McFaul	1977 (caretaker)
Richard Dinnis	1977
Bill McGarry	1977–1980
Joe Harvey	1980 (caretaker)
Arthur Cox	1980–1984
Jack Charlton	1984–1985
Willie McFaul	1985–1988
Colin Suggett	1988 (caretaker)
Jim Smith	1988–1991
Bobby Saxton	1991 (caretaker)
Ossie Ardiles	1991–1992
Kevin Keegan	1992–1997
Terry McDermott*	1997 (caretaker)
Kenny Dalglish	1997–1998
Tommy Craig**	1998 (caretaker)
Ruud Gullit	1998–1999
Steve Clarke	1999 (caretaker)
Sir Bobby Robson	1999–2004
John Carver	2004 (caretaker)
Graeme Souness	2004 –2006
Glenn Roeder	2006–2007
Nigel Pearson***	2007 (caretaker)
Sam Allardyce	2007–

(*assisted by Arthur Cox)
(**assisted by Alan Irvine)
(***assisted by Lee Clark)

Note: Frank Watt guided the club from its inception, but the side was selected by a committee during this period. Stan Seymour, meanwhile, performed the duties of team manager in two separate periods, although player selection was again officially performed by committee composed of himself and other club directors.

— THE BATTLE OF SANTIAGO —

"This is Hollywood on Tyne!"
Newcastle Chairman **Freddy Shepherd**

Tyneside in general and Newcastle United were brought to a worldwide cinema audience in 2005 with the release of the film *Goal*, the first of a planned trilogy which charted the rags to riches rise of Mexican-born footballer Santiago Munez.

Work had begun in 2004, with producer Mike Jeffries joining Bobby Robson on the St James' Park pitch to announce the project. However, footage taken that season at the Chelsea home game and Real Mallorca away UEFA Cup tie was scrapped after Mexican actor Diego Luna was replaced in the lead role.

Director Michael Winterbottom also left, replaced by Danny Cannon, who brought his film crew to Tyneside in 2005 with another Mexican-born actor, Kuno Becker, in the role of Munez.

Filming in and around the stadium took place during the home wins over Chelsea and Liverpool in Ferbruary/March 2005 – the latter game then being followed by two days of shooting in front of a 'crowd' composed of local extras.

The high level of co-operation the club gave the film makers was evident when Becker and his on-screen team-mate Gavin Harris (played by Alessandro Nivola) took to the field immediately after the final whistle at a couple of home games, dressed in replica kits.

They then proceeded to join in the authentic celebrations of the real Newcastle team, milking the genuine applause of the crowd – the scenes being captured in close up by hand held cameras.

The whole thing was then stitched together using computer-generated trickery to make empty stands appear full and intersperse real action footage of Newcastle players with specially shot re-enactments featuring the cast. Most notably, this saw Munez apparently score the winning goal in a 3–2 victory over Liverpool – although the free kick driven home at the Leazes end was actually Laurent Robert's rocket.

As Munez made his way from unpromising trialist to first team debutant/goal hero (squad number: 26), various other grounds were used.

Brentford's Griffin Park and the Loftus Road stadium of Queen's Park Rangers were used as venues for reserve games, while footage from Newcastle's victory at Fulham's Craven Cottage in May 2005 was also used.

Alan Shearer was given a brief speaking part, while most of the United first team squad at the time feature. Chairman Freddy Shepherd also pops up at one point.

Former Magpie Rob Lee plays the part of a pundit, alongside Sky commentator Martin Tyler. One of the few obvious ricks in the film, though, sees Lee demonstrate fantastic observational skills, commentating from the Newcastle press box as Munez makes his senior debut for the club – away at Fulham.

Goal had its London premiere on September 15th 2005, with a Tyneside event at 'The Gate' cinema three nights later. It then went on general UK cinema release on September 30th and subsequently worldwide. In the sequel, *Goal 2*, Santiago is sold to Real Madrid. Due to the involvement of the sportswear giant in the movies, Santiago only ever plays for teams who wear kit supplied by adidas.

— THE AGONY OF YOUTH —

Apart from their two successes in the FA Youth Cup, the Magpies have made five more losing appearances in the semi-finals:

Season	Opponent	Score/aggregate
1975/76	Wolverhampton Wanderers	lost 2–4 (1–2, 1–2)
1988/89	Manchester City	lost 1–3 (1–2, 0–1)
1998/99	Coventry City	lost 2–5 (0–4, 2–1)
2005/06	Manchester City	lost 3–4 (2–3, 1–1)
2006/07	Liverpool	lost 3–7 (2–4, 1–3)

— AD INFINITUM PART II —

A further selection of TV advertisements featuring former and future Newcastle United players and managers over the years:

McDonalds (1994)
The then 13-year-old Scott Parker played keepy-uppy in his back garden, only to be called in for his tea — at a burger bar. Paul Gascoigne and Alan Shearer also appeared in ads for the fast food company.

Milk Marketing Board (1988)
A famous ad which featured Ian Rush, with child actor Carl Rice delivering the killer line "Acrington Stanley, who are they?". The first draft of the script mentioned Tottenham Hotspur, but after the thumbs down from White Hart Lane was received, non-league Stanley were substituted.

Nescafe Carte Noire (2001)
Housewives' favourite David Ginola was drafted in to try and punt this posh instant coffee.

Persil (2004)
Michael Owen kept his England top (and image) whiter than white.

Pizza Hut (1996)
England penalty flop duo Chris Waddle and Stuart Pearce indulged in some cringe-worthy puns with new entrant to the spot-kick miss club, Gareth Southgate. Unsurprisingly, a 1998 remake with David Batty never happened. Rudd Gullit later plugged a pizza with corners . . . badly.

Renault (1996)
An ad which featured David Ginola driving his Laguna around Newcastle. A second piece of promotional work for Renault was banned by the club on insurance grounds — the French manufacturer having offered Ginola a spin at the British Touring Car Championships.

Sugar Puffs (1996)
The cereal ad showed Newcastle winning the FA Cup Final and receiving the trophy to the delight of manager Kevin Keegan, thanks to a last-minute header from the Honey Monster. A 20% drop in sales of the breakfast cereal in the North East was reported in the wake of this advert, following a boycott in the Wearside area. A mackem-led complaint was also received by the Advertising Standards Authority,

who were asked to investigate claims there was nothing remotely truthful or honest about Newcastle winning the cup.

Walkers Crisps (1995 onwards)
The High Priest of salty snack food Gary Lineker has at various times appeared alongside a crying Paul Gascoigne, Sir Bobby Robson in the guise of a guardian angel and Michael Owen (Cheese and Owen flavour).

Yellow Pages (1994)
Another outing for Bobby Robson, who was shown consulting with Graham Taylor about what to get new England boss Terry Venables for a present. A cake was the final, not particularly exciting, answer.

Apart from appearing in a number of commercial ads, Kevin Keegan also appeared in a 1976 Public Information Film, joining the likes of Alvin Stardust and Joe Bugner to promote 'The Green Cross Code' children's road safety initiative.

TV advertisers have so far failed to exploit wearside-based situations – although former mackem managers Terry Butcher and Peter Reid both appeared in the Carlsberg pub team commercial (and Reid look-a-likes once advertised PG Tips tea!)

One did slip through the net though, when Southampton boss Lawrie McMenemy (later to manage Sunderland) found himself in the proverbial, after having being convicted of a drink-driving offence. Unfortunately, he was at the time the face of Barbican alcohol-free lager. The campaign was rapidly pulled, meaning that Big Lawrie and his catchphrase, "It's great, man!", sadly disappeared from the nation's TV screens.

— CUP MARATHONS —

Now that FA Cup games are settled after a single replay, extra time or penalties if necessary, it's easy to forget that until comparatively recently, ties were played to a finish – regardless of how many games that required.

The Magpies have required three games to settle a tie on five occasions, while they've twice embarked on four-game marathons. The first of these came in the 1923/24 season, when they were drawn away to lower league Derby County in the second round. A record attendance of 27,873 attended the Baseball Ground for the first game, which ended 2–2 after the Rams recovered from being two goals behind.

The replay took place on a Wednesday afternoon in front of 50,393 fans at St James' Park and again the Magpies took a 2–0 lead only to be pegged back to 2–2 once more – Derby's cause aided by an own goal from Ted Mooney.

With extra time failing to separate the teams, a third game at a neutral ground was required and this was eventually staged at Bolton's Burnden Park after much discussion.

The following Monday afternoon 17,300 fans saw Newcastle grab an equaliser in the dying seconds of extra time for a third consecutive 2–2 draw. Derby were incensed at some alleged favouritism from referee Sam Rothwell, who awarded a dubious penalty and free-kick – both of which United converted.

After further arguments between the sides failed to reach an agreement over the venue for a fourth game, a coin was tossed and Newcastle won the right to stage the tie on Tyneside 48 hours later – with a replacement referee.

A classic encounter at St James' Park saw the Magpies come back from two goals down, a Neil Harris hat-trick providing the platform for an eventual 5–3 win in front of 32,496 spectators.

A rather less incident-packed quartet of matches in season 1988/89 saw Newcastle eventually succumb to lower league Watford in round three.

After a goalless stalemate on Tyneside the teams re-convened at Vicarage Road two nights later, United recovering from conceding an early goal to force a 2–2 draw.

The following Monday it was scoreless against at St James' Park and 48 hours later neither side could break the deadlock back in Hertfordshire.

Finally, a goal came late in extra time with an unprecedented fifth match looking inevitable, a harmless shot being deflected into his own goal by Newcastle's Glenn Roeder (who was to play and manage both sides).

The tie lasted 450 minutes – 30 more than the one with Derby County – and was an unwanted burden as Jim Smith's side struggled unsuccessfully to avoid relegation.

— NEWCASTLE LEGENDS: KEVIN KEEGAN —

Kevin Keegan: Never a dull moment

When Kevin Keegan arrived at St James' Park in August 1982, the effect he had on a club languishing in the wastelands of Division Two was instant. Amid a media frenzy, fans queued across the car park to buy season tickets and suddenly the club was alive again.

England manager Bobby Robson attended his debut, a sell-out crowd of 36,000 delighting in a 1–0 win over Queens Park Rangers thanks to a Keegan goal. Just three months earlier, by comparison, fewer than 11,000 fans had seen Rangers triumph 4–0 at Gallowgate.

However, Keegan's first season wasn't all plain sailing, as he was forced to back his under-fire manager Arthur Cox after a mid-season dip in form. Two defeats in the last ten games put the Magpies on the edge of the promotion race, but in pre-play-off days that wasn't quite enough.

The eve-of-season departure of Imre Varadi was quickly forgotten as Peter Beardsley arrived, and along with Keegan and Chris Waddle went on to score a combined total of 65 league goals in the 1983/84 promotion campaign.

A memorable farewell at home to Brighton and Hove Albion when the trio all netted was followed by a friendly with Liverpool, after which a helicopter landed on the centre circle to spirit Keegan away into retirement.

Slightly less than eight years later he returned however, to rescue a club who had lost the impetus provided by promotion and were again languishing in Division Two.

Once more the uplifting effect was instant, as Keegan brought the same spirit of infectious enthusiasm he had shown as a player to his first stab at a management. Newcastle fans responded in their droves, with a doubling of the previous home attendance to 30,000 for his first game in charge – a 3–1 win over Bristol City.

However, it's sometimes forgotten that the rest of that season was a struggle, with the threat of relegation very real until the final week.

Off-field tensions also saw further intrigue – most notably a Keegan walk-out as his team were playing Swindon Town amid accusations of broken promises by Newcastle's new owners, the Hall family.

That was all forgotten the following season, however, as the team set off at a cracking pace – winning their first eleven league games before succumbing at home to Grimsby Town. Having secured promotion and taken the title, Keegan's side then gave notice of their intention to gatecrash the Premier League with a 7–1 dismantling of Leicester City featuring hat-tricks from Andy Cole and David Kelly.

Keegan dispensed with Kelly though, re-signing Peter Beardsley to spur Cole on to a record-breaking seasonal tally of 41 goals. Cole's goals helped Newcastle to a third-place finish in the Premiership and earned the team the nickname of 'The Entertainers' (coined by Sky after a victory at Oldham Athletic in November 1993).

Sixth and second place finishes in the following two seasons kept the crowds entertained, but a visibly-aged Keegan resigned in January 1997. Various reasons were given for his shock departure, but the demands and restrictions of working for a plc remain the most plausible.

Subsequent spells in charge of Fulham, the England national side and Manchester City came to an end in 2005, since when Keegan has developed the 'Soccer Circus' project at Glasgow's Braehead retail park.

Kevin Keegan factfile
Born: Armthorpe, February 14th 1951
Newcastle career: 85 apps, 49 goals (1982–84)
Other clubs: Scunthorpe United, Liverpool, Hamburg, Southampton
International: England, 63 caps, 21 goals

— WEMBLEY MISCELLANY —

A few random facts related to the Toon's numerous Twin Towers trips:

Year	Guest of honour	Referee
1924	HRH The Duke of York	W.E. Russell
1932	King George V	Percy Harper
1951	King George VI	William Ling
1952	Winston Churchill (Prime Minister)	Arthur Ellis
1955	Queen Elizabeth II	Reg Leafe
1974	HRH Princess Anne	Gordon Kew
1976*	Duke of Norfolk	Jack Taylor
1996**	James Ross (Littlewoods Chairman)	Paul Durkin
1998	Duke and Duchess of Kent	Paul Durkin
1999	HRH Prince of Wales	Peter Jones

Note: All the above were FA Cup finals, except for *League Cup Final and **Charity Shield.

Organised community singing first became a fixture at Wembley Finals in 1927, when a TP Radcliff aka 'The Man in White' appeared on a podium to conduct the crowds. Appearing on the first songsheet was 'Abide with Me'. By the time Newcastle made their trio of successful Wembley appearances in the 1950s, the baton has been passed on to Arthur Caiger.

Incidentally, Arthur Ellis, the referee of the 1952 final went on to be better known to many as 'Uncle Arthur', resident judge of the hit TV programme *It's A Knockout!*.

In 1974, when Newcastle played Liverpool at Wembley, TV personality and *Generation Game* host Bruce Forsyth attempted to lead the singing.

— WALLSEND BOYS' CLUB —

The employees and directors of Swan Hunters Shipyard originally founded Wallsend Boys' Club in 1938 to provide recreational facilities for their apprentices and other local youngsters.

Now Swans have gone but the Boys' Club remains and still plays a key role in the local community, providing a positive influence on young people's lives.

Wallsend graduates who have gone on to join Newcastle United include:

Peter Beardsley
Ian Bogie
Lee Clark
Tony Dinning
Robbie Elliott
Chris Hedworth
Anth Lormor
Neil McDonald
David Robinson
David Roche
Alan Shearer
Eric Steele
Paul Stephenson
Alan Thompson
Steve Watson
John Watson
Jeff Wrightson

Former player Alan Shearer didn't forget his roots and Wallsend were among a large number of organisations to benefit from the proceeds of his 2006 testimonial match and other events, being awarded £15,000.

A certain other United have also indirectly benefited from the Wallsend production line, with Steve Bruce and Michael Carrick finding their way to Premiership-winning success at Old Trafford.

— GONG SHOW —

Newcastle United players and managers who have been recognised with civil or military honours include:

Recipient	Award	Year/event
Sandy Higgins	Military Medal	World War I
Tom Rowlandson	Military Cross	World War I
Donald Bell	Victoria Cross	World War I
Benny Craig	Military Medal	World War II
Ivor Allchurch	MBE	1966
Jack Charlton	OBE	1974
George Eastham	OBE	1975
Kevin Keegan	OBE	1982
Kenny Dalglish	MBE	1984
Bobby Robson	CBE	1990
Peter Beardsley	MBE	1995
Ian Rush	MBE	1996
John Barnes	MBE	1998
Stuart Pearce	MBE	1999
Alan Shearer	OBE	2001
Bobby Robson	Knighthood	2002
Les Ferdinand	MBE	2005

In addition, former Newcastle United Chairman John Hall was knighted in 1991.

Sir Bobby Robson was awarded an honorary degree by Newcastle University in 2003, becoming a Doctor of Civil Law (DCL). The same honour was then bestowed upon Alan Shearer in 2006, this time by Northumbria University.

However, the pair have some distance to go in the free degrees stakes if they're to emulate Jack Charlton. The former Newcastle United boss was honoured by the University of Limerick in 1994, by both Northumbria University and Leeds Metropolitan University in 1995 and most recently by Leeds University in 2004.

— TEENAGE KICKS PART II —

Newcastle United's second successful FA Youth Cup campaign came in the 1984/85 season, beginning with a resounding 6–0 home victory over then holders Everton. Future Magpies star Paul Gascoigne notched two in that game and scored another when Leeds United were beaten 2–0 on Tyneside in the fourth round.

The Fifth Round pitted United against Manchester City and that man Gazza was on target again as a 2–1 success was recorded. Newcastle's name came out of the hat first at the fourth time of asking, with Coventry City promptly dispatched 3–0 – two goals for Gascoigne this time round.

Into the last four and Birmingham City were beaten 2–0 at home, before a resounding 5–2 win at St Andrew's set up a final against Watford.

Just under 7,000 fans were at St James' Park to see a 0–0 stalemate, the young Hornets being captained by future Newcastle striker Malcolm Allen. There were to be no mistakes in the away leg though, Joe Allon and Paul Gascoigne delighting the travelling support in a 7,097 crowd as the team coached by Colin Suggett ran out 4–1 winners.

Seven of the final side went on to feature in the Magpies first team: Joe Allon, Paul Gascoigne, Gary Kelly, Tony Nesbit, Kevin Scott, Brian Tinnion, Jeff Wrightson. An eighth – Paul Stephenson – was on the bench. The other three players were: Stuart Dickinson, Tony Hayton and Stephen Forster.

And a further trio of players featured in ties leading up the final, these being future first team player Ian Bogie, Peter Harbach and Ian McKenzie.

— LEADING BY EXAMPLE —

Newcastle managers have taken to the field on a number of occasions in non-competitive games to show their charges just how it's done. These include:

Charlie Mitten

The former Manchester United and Fulham player celebrated the end of his first season in charge of the Magpies in May 1959 by getting his boots on. United played a three game tour of Southern Ireland, with Mitten scoring once in a 6–3 victory over Drumcondra.

Ossie Ardiles

A midweek friendly at Blyth Spartans in November 1991 gave World Cup winner Ossie the chance to pull his boots on. Ardiles was joined in the Newcastle side by his assistant manager Tony Galvin (ex-Tottenham Hotspur) and also kit man Chris Guthrie (ex- Fulham). And Ossie repeated his performance in January 1992, forming a three-man defence with Galvin and Magpies coach Derek Fazackerley as United took part game staged to inaugurate the new floodlights at local league Dunston Federation Brewery.

Kevin Keegan

Putting aside the disappointment of losing the Premiership title just days before, KK pulled on a black and white shirt at the City Ground to take part in Stuart Pearce's testimonial. The final score on an enjoyable evening was 6–5 to Pearce's Forest, with Keegan netting from the penalty spot for the black and whites.

Kevin Keegan and Kenny Dalglish

With Ruud Gullit crying off due to an unspecified illness, his two managerial predecessors both made cameo appearances for Newcastle during Peter Beardsley's testimonial game at St James' Park. For Kenny it was a chance to face his former side Celtic, although both men would have appreciated the original choice of opposition – Liverpool (who were forced to pull out due to league fixture congestion).

Ruud Gullit

Having seen his side beaten in their two previous warm-up games at Dundee United and Livingston, Ruud Gullit's patience ran out when his side trailed 0–2 at half-time away to Reading in July 1999. Withdrawing defender David Beharall from the action, Gullit emerged for the second half to try and organise his failing troops from midfield. A penalty conversion just after the hour from James Coppinger halved the arrears and a late solo effort from Paul Robinson saved the Magpies' blushes, the game ending 2–2.

Gullit then repeated the trick four nights later away at Stoke City, wearing shirt number 16 and replacing Des Hamilton after 38 minutes. He remained on the field for the rest of the evening, although in the final 30 minutes he moved further forward. One attempt at a shot saw the ball fly high and wide of the goal into an unoccupied part of the Britannia Stadium – the game being held up until a replacement ball was found.

— NO PLACE LIKE HOME —

With more and more domestic fixtures taking place in identikit stadia, here is a list of now defunct-grounds that have featured on the club's seasonal itinerary at one time or another since league football resumed in 1946. Many of them have now been replaced by housing estates, supermarkets or just levelled and left – but memories of them remain.

Opponent	Venue	Last visited
Arsenal	Highbury	2005
Bolton Wanderers	Burnden Park	1995
Bradford Park Avenue	Park Avenue	1947
Brighton and Hove Albion	Goldstone Ground	1991
Bristol Rovers	Eastville	1980
Chester City	Sealand Road	1974
Coventry City	Highfield Road	2000
Derby County	The Baseball Ground	1996
Doncaster Rovers	Belle Vue	1947
Huddersfield Town	Leeds Road	1984
Hull City	Boothferry Park	1990
Leicester City	Filbert Street	2002
Manchester City	Maine Road	2002
Middlesbrough	Ayresome Park	1992
Millwall	The Den	1993
Newport County	Somerton Park	1947
Northampton Town	The County Ground	1966
Oxford United	The Manor Ground	1992
Reading	Elm Park	1990
Scunthorpe United	The Old Showground	1974
Southampton	The Dell	2000
Stoke City	The Victoria Ground	1995
Sunderland	Roker Park	1996
Swansea City	Vetch Field	1983
Walsall	Fellows Park	1975
Wigan Athletic	Springfield Park	1954
Wimbledon	Plough Lane	1989

Note: Dates given are of the last competitive first team game Newcastle played at the venue. The Magpies have appeared in friendlies at other grounds which no longer exist but never played competitively there – hence their omission from the list.

— "HELLO NEWCASTLE!" —

Before 1982, the only live musical performances at St James' Park had come from local brass bands entertaining the crowd.

However on June 23rd of that year, a date on the Rolling Stones European Tour marked the debut of the ground as a live popular music venue. Messrs Jagger, Richards, Wood, Wyman and Watts performed on a stage erected across the Leazes End goalmouth with fans in both stands, standing on the matted pitch and spread across the Gallowgate End.

Support act for that gig was American combo, The J Geils Band, while a year later on July 15th 1984, local lads Lindisfarne and Mexican guitarist Carlos Santana opened for Bob Dylan, in town as part of his European Tour.

1985 then saw Bruce Springsteen and The E Street Band perform at the stadium on both 4th and 5th June as part of the 'Born In The USA' tour. Springsteen then moved on to mainland Europe, playing gigs at a number of outdoor venues including football stadia in Rotterdam, Munich and Milan that have all played host to Newcastle in European football fixtures.

A year later and July 9th 1986 saw Queen entertain the crowds, supported by Status Quo. A third act had been due to play, but an accident on the A1 delayed the arrival of the equipment and road crew for the Australian rockers INXS.

After a four year hiatus, the Rolling Stones returned to the stadium on July 18th 1990, as part of their 'Urban Jungle' tour. Support this time came from US group Dan Reed Network and English rockers The Quireboys – the latter who included Tynesider Spike on lead vocals.

It took another 16 years before live music returned to the venue, when Bryan Adams appeared on June 6th 2006, supported by Beverley Knight. With the stadium having been reconstructed in the intervening years, the stage was constructed to face the North West corner, with fans occupying both seats and a standing area in front of the stage.

June 25th 2007 then saw Rod Stewart in Toon, with support coming from The Pretenders.

Local band Lindisfarne made a return visit to St James' Park on May 7th 1993, playing for the crowd attending the final game of the season, against Leicester City. Promoting their album *Elvis Live on the Moon*, they played from a temporary stage erected on the partly-constructed new Leazes End Stand.

— CAN YOU SPELL THAT PLEASE? —

Some of the more elongated formal names of Newcastle players have included:

Full name	AKA
Faustino Hernan Hinestroza **Asprilla**	Tino
Carlos Daniel Lobo **Cordone**	Daniel
Diego Antonio **Gavilan** Zarate	Diego
Fransiscus Leonardus Albertus **Koenen**	Frans
Elena Sierra **Marcelino**	Martha
Obafemi Akinwunmi **Martins**	Oba
Francisco Ernandi Lima da Silva **Mirandinha**	Mira
Oguchialu Chilioke **Onyewu**	Gooch
Nolberto Albino **Solano** Todco	Nobby
Hugo Miguel Ferreira **Viana**	Hugo

In January 1997, United announced that the Portuguese central defender Raul Oliveira had passed a medical and was set to sign on loan from Farense. However, the deal fell through and Oliveira later appeared briefly for Bradford City, before returning to Portugal. The player's full name was: Raul Miguel Silva da Fonseca Castanheira de Oliveira.

At the opposite end of the scale, the club took goalkeeper An Qi on trial in December 2002 from Chinese club Dalian Shide, but didn't offer him a contract.

— IT'S A FAMILY AFFAIR I —

Brothers who have played for Newcastle United over the years include:

Appleby   Teessiders Matty and Richie were at St James' Park together in the early 1990s, but while the elder Matty appeared for the first team in defence, the younger Richie never got the chance to show his midfield skills in a competitive senior game. However, the duo were selected in the same team by Kevin Keegan in Anglo-Italian Cup ties away to Bari and at home to Cesena in 1992.

Caldwell   Despite playing together at junior and reserve level, the nearest central defenders Steve and Gary got to partnering each other in the first team came when Sir Bobby Robson brought them both off the bench during a testimonial match at West Bromwich Albion in 2001. After the pair had left

United, they appeared together competitively for the first time at senior level when both were selected for Scotland in a World Cup qualifier away to Moldova in October 2004.

King   Amble-born goalkeeper Ray and his elder striker brother George were both at Gallowgate when World War II ended but never played in the first team together.

Robledo   Chilean pair George and Eduardo ('Ted') were signed from Barnsley in January 1949, United taking the younger left-sided midfielder Ted in order to capture the signature of his striker brother. The brothers appeared together for the first time in a Newcastle shirt on the last day of 1949, away to Aston Villa.

Withe   Merseyside-born duo Peter and Chris were on the books at St James' Park together in the 1970s, but the younger Chris (a defender) only made his first team debut the season after the older Peter (a striker) had left.

The following sets of brothers were on the club's books together, but only the Kennedy brothers both appeared in the football league.

Ameobi	Shola and Tomi
Elliott	Robbie and John
Hislop	Shaka and Kona
Howie	Jimmy and David
Keating	Bert and Reg
Kennedy	Alan and Keith
Lindsay	Billy and James
Mitten	John and Charles junior
Rutherford	Jackie and Andrew
Smith	'Tot', George and Robert
Wilson	Joe and Glenn

— NEWCASTLE LEGENDS: STAN SEYMOUR —

Stan Seymour: Gave his life to Newcastle United

As captain, manager, director and Vice-President, Seymour served Newcastle United in three spells over a period of almost 70 years.

The man known as 'Mister Newcastle' thanks to his achievements on and off the field was initially discarded by the Magpies as a teenage amateur player before World War I, returning to play local football for Shildon.

After a brief spell at Bradford City, Seymour's career took off after some impressive displays for Greenock Morton, before a move to Newcastle followed in May 1920.

The return on the £2,500 fee was instant as Seymour marked his debut with a goal on the opening day of the season, although his side only managed a 1–1 home draw with West Bromwich Albion.

Four solid seasons in the Newcastle side at outside-left brought successive top ten finishes, culminating in a 2–0 victory in the 1924 FA Cup Final, where Seymour scored the second goal in the dying minutes of the club's Wembley debut.

Seymour's finest campaign, however, came in 1926/27 when he was an ever-present in Newcastle's championship-winning side, scoring 18 goals in the process – the last of which gave his team the 1–1 draw that clinched the title away to West Ham United.

He retired from playing two seasons later, his final appearance coming at Gallowgate against Arsenal in October 1928.

In 1937 Seymour was invited to join the Newcastle board of directors. He accepted, giving up his sideline of reporting on matches for newspapers but retaining ownership of the sports shop he'd established in the city.

After the war years intervened, Seymour set about reconstructing the side which achieved promotion back to the First Division at the second attempt in 1948.

Having handed over nominal control of team affairs to George Martin, Seymour took over again when Martin defected to Aston Villa in 1950, presiding over two Wembley FA Cup Final successes.

A dip in results, however, led to Seymour being persuaded by his fellow directors to try another team manager, Duggie Livingstone arriving in December 1954.

He was to last barely a year though, with Seymour famously over-ruling him before the 1955 FA Cup Final, when the name of Jackie Milburn failed to appear on the first Newcastle teamsheet submitted to the directors.

Seymour remained at St James' Park while Charlie Mitten and Norman Smith were tried in the manager's job. However, his masterstroke proved to be bringing Joe Harvey back to Tyneside in 1962 – the former Magpies captain having been overlooked for the post when Mitten was appointed, moving on to learn his trade at Workington.

With Harvey's departure in 1975, Seymour retired as a director the following year at the age of 83. He passed away two years later, having seen his son join the board – although he didn't live to see Stan Seymour junior emulate his father and become chairman.

George Stanley Seymour factfile
Born: Kelloe, County Durham, 16th May 1893
Died: December 24th 1978
Newcastle career: 1920–29
Other clubs: Shildon Town, Coxhoe, Bradford City, Greenock Morton

— FA CUP HAT-TRICK HEROES —

Seventeen players have scored FA Cup hat-tricks for Newcastle, the last being Paul Kitson against Swansea City back in 1994. The full list is:

Player	Season	Opponent
Bill Appleyard	1907/08	Grimsby Town (h)
George Wilson	1908/09	Clapton Orient (h)
Albert Shepherd	1910/11	Bury (h)
Neil Harris	1923/24	Derby County (h)
Hughie Gallacher	1926/27	Notts County (h)
Tom McDonald	1926/27	Notts County (h)
Jimmy Richardson	1929/30	Clapton Orient (h)
Hughie Gallacher	1929/30	Brighton & Hove Albion (h)
Duncan Hutchison	1930/31	Nottingham Forest (h)
Jimmy Richardson	1931/32	Southport (n)
Charlie Wayman	1946/47	Southampton (h)
Jackie Milburn	1949/50	Oldham Athletic (a)
Jackie Milburn	1951/52	Portsmouth (a)
Len White	1957/58	Plymouth Argyle (a)
Duncan Neale	1960/61	Fulham (h)
Wyn Davies	1966/67	Coventry City (a)
Paul Kitson	1994/95	Swansea City (h)

In addition, Andy Aitken netted four times in an FA Cup qualifying round home tie against local side Willington Athletic in season 1897/98.

— INDIVIDUAL LEAGUE CUP SCORING FEATS —

Player	Season	Opponent	Goals scored
Alan Gowling	1975/76	Southport (h)	4
Malcolm Macdonald	1973/74	Doncaster Rovers (h)	3
Malcolm Macdonald	1974/75	Queens Park Rangers (h)	3
Gavin Peacock	1991/92	Crewe Alexandra (a)	3
Andy Cole	1993/94	Notts County (h)	3
Andy Cole	1993/94	Notts County (a)	3
Craig Bellamy	2001/02	Brentford (h)	3

— TWIN TOWERS PART III —

As well as their various cup final and semi-final outings, a Newcastle side has also appeared at Wembley on another occasion, as part of The Football League Centenary celebrations of 1988.

The Mercantile Credit Football Festival was a two-day knock-out event involving 16 teams, who played each other in limited duration (20 minutes each way) games on a reduced size pitch.

Qualification for the event was based on the number of league points gained during a three month period earlier in the season from Divisions One to Four – eight clubs joining from the First, four from the Second and two each from Divisions Three and Four.

The event took place over a Saturday and Sunday when no league games were scheduled. And in what was already the second game of the day, Newcastle kicked off at 10.50am before a sparsely populated Wembley against Liverpool.

Newcastle fielded a side including the likes of Gary Kelly, Paul Gascoigne, Brian Tinnion, Glenn Roeder, Paul Goddard, Mirandhina, Neil McDonald and Michael O'Neill while John Bailey was an unused substitute. After a 0–0 draw, the tie was settled on penalties – but in a change to the usual practice, these were sudden death from the off. Steve McMahon took the first Liverpool spot kick, only for Kelly to parry it over the crossbar. That meant that Newcastle only had to score to go through and McDonald duly obliged to give the club a rare Wembley victory to savour.

In the second game the Magpies came back down to earth with a bump though, losing 2–0 to Tranmere Rovers of Division Four. The side from Birkenhead netted through John Morrissey and an Ian Muir penalty and Toon misery was complete when the Rovers keeper saved a penalty from Mirandinha.

Tranmere were so up for it that they'd even recorded a tune for their Wembley bow (*We are the Rovers* by Don Woods) and had beaten Division One side Wimbledon in their first game. With many of the 1,000 or so Newcastle followers there having purchased weekend tickets, the Sunday saw them trudge back again for a further day of pointless games not involving their own club.

Nottingham Forest were the eventual winners of the competition, but their manager Brian Clough was so uninterested in proceedings that he declined to attend.

— DREAM STARTS II —

The only Newcastle player to have made his debut as a substitute and scored was Alex Mathie in 1993.

George Dalton netted within six minutes of his debut, at home to Leicester City in 1961. Unfortunately it was an own goal.

Aside from the select few players who scored at least a hat trick on their first competitive appearance for Newcastle, a number of others have also marked their debut in memorable style by bagging two goals:

Year	Player	Opponent/venue
1906	Finlay Speedie	The Wednesday (h)
1907	George Wilson	Liverpool (a)
1925	Hughie Gallacher	Everton (h)
1946	George Stobbart	Coventry City (h)
1946	Jackie Milburn	Barnsley (h)
1958	Arthur Bottom	Everton (a)
1958	Ivor Allchurch	Leicester City (h)
1960	Duncan Neale	Fulham (h)
1998	Duncan Ferguson	Wimbledon (h)

— IT'S A FAMILY AFFAIR II —

The following families have had fathers and sons who have represented Newcastle:

Edgar   Goalkeeper Eddie made one first team appearance in 1976 before emigrating to Canada. His son David (a defender) was born in Kitchener, Ontario but moved to Newcastle and came through the ranks to make his first team debut in December 2006.

Wilson   Defender Joseph and his centre forward son Carl both made a single league appearance for Newcastle's first team – the latter the only one of seven footballing brothers to emulate his father.

Other fathers and sons who have both been on the club's books, include:

Cahill	Tommy and Tommy Junior
Gallacher	Hughie, Hughie junior and Matt
McDermott	Terry and Neale
McDonald*	James and Neil

135

Nattrass	Irving and Paul
Niblo	Tom and Alan
Seymour	Stan and Colin
Swinburne	Tom, Alan and Trevor
Wharton	Kenny and Paul
Wrightson	Jeff and Kieran

Note: Second (and third) named didn't play first team football for the club except*, where the father failed but the son succeeded.

— MANX MAGS —

Back in the 1980s when competitive fixtures for Newcastle got no more exotic than trips to Wales, friendly tours provided some variety and a change of scenery for the more intrepid supporter. However, the loyalty of the most diehard Magpie follower was tested when the club opted to participate in the Isle of Man Tournament as part of their pre-season programme in both 1985 and 1986.

Newcastle's first appearance in the tournament coincided with a summer season on the island from singer Tony Christie, while the following year featured cabaret delights in the shape of Les Dennis, Max Boyce and Rod Hull and Emu!

1985:

Venue	Fixture/result	Newcastle scorer(s)
Douglas	Leicester City 3 Newcastle 2	Peter Beardsley, George Reilly
Ramsey	Blackburn Rovers 2 Newcastle 1	Paul Gascoigne
Castletown	Wigan Athletic 1 Newcastle 4	Neil McDonald 2, Glenn Roeder, Peter Beardsley

1986:

Venue	Fixture/result	Newcastle scorer(s)
Douglas	Blackburn Rovers 2 Newcastle 2	Paul Gascoigne, Neil McDonald
Castletown	Portsmouth 2 Newcastle 2	Neil McDonald, Joe Allon
Castletown	Isle of Man XI 1 Newcastle 5	Ian Stewart, Peter Beardsley Joe Allon 2, Paul Ferris

— BIG DAY OUT IN THE NORTH —

A selection of crucial final fixtures at St James' Park over the years – crucial for the opposition that is:

April 1903 Requiring a victory on Tyneside to retain the First Division title, Sunderland blew their big chance by losing 1–0 to Newcastle. The Wearsiders' defeat meant they finished third behind title winners The Wednesday and runners-up Aston Villa.

May 1926 Having lost the FA Cup final on the previous Saturday, Manchester City arrived at Gallowgate needing to avoid defeat in order to secure their First Division status. Sadly for them, the game finished in a 3–2 victory for Newcastle with City missing a penalty.

April 1949 A resounding 5–0 away success by Portsmouth confirmed the status of the south coast team as Division One champions, Jack Froggatt leading the way with a hat-trick.

April 1962 The start of the Don Revie era of success came at St James' Park as Leeds United won 3–0 to banish any fear of relegation to Division Three (although other results meant they were safe regardless of the score). The visitors led at the interval thanks to an own goal, with second half efforts from Billy McAdams and Albert Johanneson securing victory. Just three years later Leeds were runners-up in Division One.

May 1968 Manchester City were pressed all the way by the home side before triumphing 4–3 to lift the First Division title, thanks to goals from Neil Young (2), Mike Summerbee and Francis Lee.

May 1979 The penultimate home game of the season saw the gate increase by some 19,000 to over 28,000 as Malcolm Allison brought his Brighton and Hove Albion side to Tyneside. Having been at St James' Park the previous Wednesday to watch Newcastle beat Bristol Rovers 3–0, The Seagulls raced into a similar lead before the interval after Brian Horton, Peter Ward and Gerry Ryan all netted.

And although Alan Shoulder reduced the arrears after the break, Brighton were never in danger of losing the points that confirmed their promotion to Division One for the first time in their history, behind title winners Crystal Palace.

— PREMIERSHIP DISMISSALS —

Prior to the start of the 2007/08 season, 44 players had been dismissed while appearing for Newcastle United in their 540 Premiership fixtures. Four of those decisions were subsequently rescinded. The full list is:

Year	Player	Fixture/venue	Result
1993	Pavel Srnicek	Coventry City (a)	lost 1–2
1994	Pavel Srnicek	Leicester City (a)	won 3–1
1994	Philippe Albert	Liverpool (h)	drew 1–1
1995	Robert Lee	Everton (a)	lost 0–2
1995	Pavel Srnicek	Tottenham Hotspur (h)	drew 3–3
1995	John Beresford	Everton (h)	won 1–0
1996	David Batty	Chelsea (a)	drew 1–1
1997	Keith Gillespie	Arsenal (a)	won 1–0
1997	David Batty	Aston Villa (h)	won 1–0
1997	David Batty	Derby County (a)	lost 0–1
1998	David Batty	Blackburn Rovers (a)	lost 0–1
1998	Nicos Dabizas	Arsenal (a)	lost 0–3
1998	Stuart Pearce	West Ham United (h)	lost 0–3
1998	Didi Hamann	Liverpool (a)	lost 2–4
1999	Nicos Dabizas	Charlton Athletic (a)	drew 2–2
1999	Alan Shearer	Aston Villa (h)	lost 0–1
1999	Nicos Dabizas	Manchester United (a)	lost 1–5
1999	Warren Barton	Coventry City (a)	lost 1–4
2000	Warren Barton	Derby County (h)	won 3–2
2001	Nolberto Solano	Tottenham Hotspur (a)	lost 2–4
2001	Kieron Dyer	Tottenham Hotspur (a)	lost 2–4
2001	Nolberto Solano	Ipswich Town (a)	lost 0–1
2001	Gary Speed*	Aston Villa (h)	won 3–0
2001	Alan Shearer*	Charlton Athletic (a)	drew 1–1
2001	Craig Bellamy*	Arsenal (a)	won 3–1
2002	Nicos Dabizas	Blackburn Rovers (a)	lost 2–5
2003	Laurent Robert	Arsenal (h)	drew 1–1
2003	Andy Griffin	Fulham (a)	lost 1–2
2003	Laurent Robert	Everton (a)	drew 2–2
2003	Andy O'Brien	Chelsea (a)	lost 0–5
2004	Andy O'Brien	Aston Villa (a)	drew 0–0
2004	Lee Bowyer	Liverpool (a)	lost 1–3
2005	Lee Bowyer	Aston Villa (h)	lost 0–3
2005	Kieron Dyer	Aston Villa (h)	lost 0–3
2005	Steven Taylor	Aston Villa (h)	lost 0–3
2005	Shola Ameobi	Everton (a)	lost 0–2

2005	Jermaine Jenas*	Arsenal (a)	lost 0–2
2005	Scott Parker	Fulham (a)	drew 1–1
2005	Steven Taylor	Blackburn Rovers (a)	won 3–0
2005	Lee Bowyer	Liverpool (a)	lost 0–2
2006	Celestine Babayaro	Aston Villa (a)	won 2–1
2006	Jean-Alain Boumsong	Liverpool (h)	lost 1–3
2006	Stephen Carr	Chelsea (h)	won 1–0
2006	Titus Bramble	Everton (h)	drew 1–1

* Subsequently rescinded

Saturday April 2nd 2005 remains Newcastle's blackest day in the Premiership, with Bowyer and Dyer dismissed for fighting with each other in the 82nd minute of the game. That reduced the Magpies to eight men, Steven Taylor having been red carded nine minutes previously by referee Barry Knight for deliberate handball.

In addition, there has been one instance of a Newcastle player being red carded while not on the field of play. This came in October 2005 at St James' Park when a case of mistaken identity saw Scott Parker wrongly yellow carded. When the error was realised post-match, the booking was transferred to the guilty party, Stephen Carr, who had already been booked in the game and was subsequently banned.

— SINGLETOONS —

The following 60 players made one league start for Newcastle United but never featured in any other competitive game for the club.

Name	Year	Name	Year
J W Barr	1893	M. Keir	1893
John Patten	1893	Alex Ramsay	1893
Isaac Ryder	1893	William Simm	1893
Haynes	1895	Thomas Blyth	1897
John Allen	1898	Archie Mowatt	1898
George Mole	1900	Daniel Pattinson	1902
Ord Richardson	1902	Bob Benson	1903
Hugh Bolton	1905	Tom Rowlandson	1905
R.E. Rutherford	1906	George Hedley	1907
Ben Nicholson	1907	Noel Brown	1908
Bob Blanthorne	1908	William Hughes	1908
Alex McCulloch	1908	Jack Thomas	1912
Jack Alderson	1913	Thomas Grey	1914

Tom Cairns	1915	John Soulsby	1915
Alex Rainnie	1920	John Thain	1921
John Archibald	1922	Allan Taylor	1925
Billy Halliday	1927	Stan Barber	1928
Robert Bradley	1928	Joe Wilson	1929
Ike Keen	1930	James Robinson	1931
Joe Ford	1932	Tom McBain	1932
David Smith	1936	John Shiel	1937
George Bradley	1938	Dominic Kelly	1939
Ron Anderson	1947	Albert Clark	1948
Andy Graver	1950	Alex Gaskell	1953
Bill Redhead	1956	Chris Harker	1958
Carl Wilson	1958	Grant Malcolm	1959
George Watkin	1962	Les O'Neil	1963
John Hope	1969	Keith Kennedy	1972
Tony Bell	1974	Rob McKinnon	1985*
Paul Moran	1991*		

(*substituted during the game)

In addition, five players made their only Newcastle appearance as substitutes in league games:

Martin Gorry	1977
Keith Mulgrove	1978
Kevin Pugh	1981
John Watson	1991
James Coppinger	2000

In the various cup competitions Newcastle have been involved in, the various incarnations of the League Cup have given five players the chance to register their sole first class appearance as a Magpie:

Billy Wilson	1961
Derek Craig	1971
Phil Leaver	1980
Justin Fashanu	1991 (as sub)
Steve Guppy	1994 (as sub)

Two more players made their sole outing to date in the UEFA Cup:

Lewis Guy	2004 (as sub)
Tim Krul	2006

And finally, the FA Cup saw one debutant who never appeared again:

Eddie Edgar	1976

Perhaps the most luckless trio of 'singletoons' are Thomas Blyth, George Mole and Daniel Pattinson – who all marked their only game for the club by scoring a goal.

James Coppinger's Premiership experience consisted of 11 minutes at home to Chelsea, while fellow striker Lewis Guy played for exactly the same duration at home to Sporting Lisbon in the UEFA Cup. The pair subsequently played together when both moved on to Doncaster Rovers.

— CLOSE BUT . . . —

Players who were selected as first team substitutes for Newcastle United but failed to make a competitive senior appearance include:

Player	Season(s) selected
Terry Melling	1965/66
Terry Johnson	1968/69
Dave Clarke	1968/69
Billy Coulson	1971/72
Brian Reid	1993/94
Jason Drysdale	1994/95
Paul Barrett	1996/97
Stuart Elliott	1996/97, 1997/98
David Terrier	1997/98
Ralf Keidel	1997/98
Brian Pinas	1997/98
Lionel Perez	1998/99, 1999/00
Peter Keen	1998/99
Gary Caldwell	1999/00, 2000/01
Stuart Green	1999/00, 2001/02
Tony Caig	2002/03, 2003/04, 2004/05
Bradley Orr	2003/04
Kris Gate	2005/06
James Troisi	2006/07
Kazenga LuaLua	2006/07
Fraser Forster	2006/07

— ATLANTIC CROSSING —

A number of players who also featured for Newcastle have given service
to 'soccer' clubs in The United States of America, since the round
ball game was popularised in the 1880s:

Player	Club	Year joined
Jerry Best	Providence Clamdiggers	1924
Jerry Best	New Bedford Whalers	1926
Jerry Best	Fall River Marksmen	1929
Jerry Best	Pawtucket Rangers	1929
Viv Busby	Tulsa Roughnecks	1980
Paul Cannell	Washington Diplomats	1978
Paul Cannell	Memphis Rogues	1979
Paul Cannell	Detroit Express	1981
Franz Carr	Pittsburgh Riverhounds	2000
Paul Dalglish	Houston Dynamo	2006
Ian Davies	Detroit Express	1978
George Eastham	Cleveland Stokers	1967
Eddie Edgar	New York Cosmos	1979
Justin Fashanu	Los Angeles Heat	1988
Alan Foggon	Rochester Lancers	1976
Alan Foggon	Hartford BiCentennials	1976
Howard Gayle	Dallas Sidekicks	1986
Steve Guppy	DC United	2005
Steve Hardwick	Detroit Express	1978
Bryan Harvey	New York Americans	1962
Gordon Hindson	Hartford Bicentennials	1976
Shaka Hislop	Baltimore Blast	1992
Shaka Hislop	FC Dallas	2006
Trevor Hockey	San Diego Jaws	1976
Trevor Hockey	Las Vegas Quicksilvers	1977
Trevor Hockey	San Jose Earthquakes	1977
Pat Howard	Portland Timbers	1978
Steve Howey	New England Revolution	2004
Rocky Hudson	Fort Lauderdale Strikers	1978
Rocky Hudson	Minnesota Strikers	1986
Mike Mahoney	Chicago Sting	1978
Mike Mahoney	California Surf	1979
Mike Mahoney	Los Angeles Lazers	1982
Mick Martin	Vancouver Whitecaps	1984
Kenny Mitchell	Tulsa Roughnecks	1978
David McCreery	Tulsa Roughnecks	1981

John McGuigan	New York Americans	1962
Michael O'Neill	Portland Timbers	2001
Graham Oates	Detroit Express	1978
Graham Oates	California Surf	1981
Andy Parkinson	Philadelphia Fury	1980
Andy Parkinson	Team America	1983
Andy Parkinson	New York Cosmos	1984
Andy Parkinson	Fort Lauderdale Strikers	1988
Willie Penman	Seattle Sounders	1974
Keith Robson	Team Hawaii	1977
Eric Ross	Detroit Cougars	1967
Liam Tuohy	Boston Rovers	1967
Nigel Walker	San Diego Sockers	1982
Peter Withe	Portland Timbers	1975

In addition, a smaller number of Magpies have found themselves playing the game in Canada over the years:

Player	Club	Year joined
Peter Beardsley	Vancouver Whitecaps	1981
Alex Caie	Westmount	circa 1914
Alex Caie	Sons of Scotland	circa 1914
Tony Caig	Vancouver Whitecaps	2006
Paul Cannell	Calgary Boomers	1980
Tommy Casey	Inter Roma	1963
Alex Cropley	Toronto Blizzard	1981
Eddie Edgar	London City	1980
Justin Fashanu	Edmonton Brickmen	1988
Rocky Hudson	Edmonton Brickmen	1987
Peter Kelly	London City	1981
Andy Parkinson	Montreal Manic	1981
Craig Robson	Vancouver Whitecaps	2003
Colin Suggett	Vancouver Canadians	1967
Andy Walker	Toronto Blizzard	1983
Kenny Wharton	Winnipeg Furies	1990

Both Graeme Souness (Montreal Olympique as a player) and Sir Bobby Robson (Vancouver Royals as manager) had spells in Canada.

— ONLY THE LOANEES —

Players who have moved from other clubs for temporary stints in a Newcastle shirt include:

Player	Loaned from	Year
Viv Busby	Luton Town	1971
Alex Cropley	Aston Villa	1980
Alan Brown	Sunderland	1981
David Mills	West Bromwich Albion	1982
Howard Gayle	Liverpool	1982
Martin Thomas	Bristol Rovers	1983
Ian Baird	Southampton	1984
Dave McKellar	Hibernian	1986
Darren Bradshaw	York City	1989
Tommy Gaynor	Nottingham Forest	1990
Dave Mitchell	Chelsea	1991
Paul Moran	Tottenham Hotspur	1991
Andy Walker	Celtic	1991
Gavin Maguire	Portsmouth	1991
Paul Bodin	Crystal Palace	1991
Terry Wilson	Nottingham Forest	1992
Brian Kilcline	Oldham Athletic	1992
Brian Reid	Glasgow Rangers	1994
Tommy Wright	Manchester City	1999
Helder	Deportivo La Coruna	1999
Wayne Quinn	Sheffield United	2001
Sylvain Distin	Paris St.Germain	2001
Michael Bridges	Leeds United	2004
Giuseppe Rossi	Manchester United	2006
Oguchi Onyewu	Standard Liege	2007

Of these players, Mills, Thomas, Bradshaw, Kilcline and Quinn were ultimately signed by Newcastle on permanent contracts. Attempts were made to sign both Brown and Distin – the former returning to Wearside after allegedly failing a medical amid rumours the Magpies lacked the funds to fund the deal.

Distin, on the other hand, opted not to prolong his stay at Gallowgate despite offers to do so and a £4m transfer fee having been agreed with his club. He moved on to newly-promoted Manchester City, with Newcastle lodging a formal complaint of 'tapping up' allegations. Even since then, Distin has been the target for vocal abuse from Newcastle supporters when he has played for City against his former club.

One player who was never in danger of being offered a contract was Paul Moran, who made one ill-starred appearance at home to Wolverhampton Wanderers and was soon on his way back to White Hart Lane.

— BRIEF ENCOUNTERS I —

A selection of some of the more exotic players who spent time on trial with Newcastle United but never appeared for the club competitively:

Player	Country of Birth
Bernard Allou	Ivory Coast
Teoman Arika	Turkey
Paulo Baier	Brazil
Jean-Hugues Ateba Bilayi	Cameroon
Jorge Bohme	Germany
Dries Boussatta	Morocco
Pierre Boya	Cameroon
Erol Bulut	Germany
Francesco Coco	Italy
Costas Costa	Cyprus
George Christouplos	Australia
Garra Dembele	Mali
John Doyle	USA
Jan Eriksson	Sweden
Carlos Sierra Fumero	Spain
Wael Gomaa	Egypt
Sergei Gurenko	Belarus
Ove Hansen	Denmark
Esteban Herrera	Argentina
Martin Hidalgo	Peru
Leo Houtsanan	Finland
Thomas Huschbeck	Germany
Sami Hyppia	Finland
Rodney Jack	Jamaica
Sun Jihai	China

— CLUB TRIPS —

Newcastle United have regularly embarked upon pre and post-season tours to an array of overseas destinations, where they've played numerous friendly matches:

Year	Destination
1904	Denmark
1905	Bohemia
1906	Bohemia
1907	Germany
1909	Denmark
1911	Germany/Switzerland
1913	Denmark
1921	Spain/France
1922	Norway/Sweden/Denmark
1924	Spain
1927	Holland
1929	Austria/Czechoslovakia/Hungary
1932	France/Germany
1946	Norway/Sweden
1949	USA/Canada
1952	Southern Africa
1955	West Germany
1956	Spain/West Germany
1958	Spain/Romania
1959	Southern Ireland
1959	Spain (Mallorca)*
1960	West Germany/Yugoslavia/Spain
1965	Denmark/West Germany
1970	USA/Canada
1972	Thailand/Hong Kong/Iran
1976	Norway
1977	Malta
1977	Holland*
1978	Sweden*
1980	Sweden*
1982	Portugal (Madeira)*
1983	Malaysia/Thailand/Japan
1983	West Germany/Greece*
1985	New Zealand/Fiji
1988	Sweden*
1989	Sweden*
1990	Hungary (Budapest)*

1991	Sweden*
1994	Finland*
1996	Thailand/Singapore/Japan*
1999	Holland*
2000	Trinidad/Tobago
2000	USA*
2002	Holland*
2003	Malaysia*
2004	Thailand/Hong Kong*

Note: all trips were post-season except those marked* which were pre-season.

— BRIEF ENCOUNTERS II —

A further selection of overseas players who spent time on trial with Newcastle United but never made a competitive appearance for the club:

Player	Country of Birth
Hamed Kavianpour	Iran
Joonas Kolka	Finland
Yoann Lachor	France
Dennis Lawrence	Trinidad
Erwin Lemmens	Belgium
Dragan Lukic	Yugoslavia
Ernest Mtawali	Malawi
Markus Munch	Germany
Nicki Bille Nielsen	Denmark
Victor Nogueira	Portugal
Massimo Oddo	Italy
Isaac Okoronkwo	Nigeria
Pietro Parente	Italy
Pablo Paz	Argentina
Bruno Pereira	Portugal
Bachirou Salou	Togo
Christian Schwegler	Switzerland
Diaby Sekana	Ivory Coast
Tariq	Libya
Shalom Tikva	Israel
Diego Tur	Denmark
Frank Wiblishauser	Germany
Ray Xuerub	Malta
Marc Ziegler	Germany
Chris Zoricich	New Zealand

— EXPERIENCE REQUIRED —

The following players who managed Newcastle at some stage in their career but didn't play for the club participated in the World Cup finals:

Year	Host	Player	Nation
1954	Switzerland	Bill McGarry	England
1958	Sweden	Bobby Robson	England
1962	Chile	Bobby Robson	England (non-playing)
1966	England	Jack Charlton	England
1970	Mexico	Jack Charlton	England
1974	West Germany	Kenny Dalglish	Scotland
1978	Argentina	Osvaldo Ardiles	Argentina
1978	Argentina	Graeme Souness	Scotland
1978	Argentina	Kenny Dalglish	Scotland
1982	Spain	Kenny Dalglish	Scotland
1982	Spain	Osvaldo Ardiles	Argentina
1982	Spain	Graeme Souness	Scotland
1986	Mexico	Graeme Souness	Scotland
1990	Italy	Ruud Gullit	Netherlands

— NEWCASTLE UNITED'S
LEAGUE RECORD 1893–2007 —

SEASON	(DIV)	Home						Away						
		P	W	D	L	F	A	W	D	L	F	A	Pts	Pos
1893/94	2	28	12	1	1	44	10	3	5	6	22	29	36	4th
1894/95	2	30	11	1	3	51	28	1	2	12	21	56	27	10th
1895/96	2	30	14	0	1	57	14	2	2	11	16	36	34	5th
1896/97	2	30	13	1	1	42	13	4	0	11	14	39	35	5th
1897/98	2	30	14	0	1	43	10	7	3	5	21	22	45	2nd
														(Promoted)
1898/99	1	34	9	3	5	33	18	2	5	10	16	30	30	13th
1899/00	1	34	10	5	2	34	15	3	5	9	19	28	36	5th
1900/01	1	34	10	5	2	27	13	4	5	8	15	24	38	6th
1901/02	1	34	11	3	3	41	14	3	6	8	7	20	37	3rd
1902/03	1	34	12	1	4	31	11	2	3	12	10	40	32	14th
1903/04	1	34	12	3	2	31	13	6	3	8	27	32	42	4th
1904/05	1	34	14	1	2	41	12	9	1	7	31	21	48	1st
														(Champions)
1905/06	1	38	12	4	3	49	23	6	3	10	25	25	43	4th
1906/07	1	38	18	1	0	51	12	4	6	9	23	34	51	1st
														(Champions)
1907/08	1	38	11	4	4	41	24	4	8	7	24	30	42	4th
1908/09	1	38	14	1	4	32	20	10	4	5	33	21	53	1st
														(Champions)
1909/10	1	38	11	3	5	33	22	8	4	7	37	34	45	4th
1910/11	1	38	8	7	4	37	18	7	3	9	24	25	40	8th
1911/12	1	38	10	4	5	37	25	8	4	7	27	25	44	3rd
1912/13	1	38	8	5	6	30	23	5	3	11	17	24	34	14th
1913/14	1	38	9	6	4	27	18	4	5	10	12	30	37	11th
1914/15	1	38	8	4	7	29	23	3	6	10	17	25	32	15th
1915/19						FIRST WORLD WAR								
1919/20	1	42	11	5	5	31	13	6	4	11	13	26	43	8th
1920/21	1	42	14	3	4	43	18	6	7	8	23	27	50	5th
1921/22	1	42	11	5	5	36	19	7	5	9	23	26	46	7th
1922/23	1	42	13	6	2	31	11	5	6	10	14	26	48	4th
1923/24	1	42	13	5	3	40	21	4	5	12	20	33	42	9th
1924/25	1	42	11	6	4	43	18	5	10	6	18	24	48	6th
1925/26	1	42	13	3	5	59	33	3	7	11	25	42	42	10th
1926/27	1	42	19	1	1	64	20	6	5	10	32	38	56	1st
														(Champions)
1927/28	1	42	9	7	5	49	41	6	6	9	30	40	43	9th

Season	Div	P	W	D	L	F	A	W	D	L	F	A	Pos
1928/29	1	42	15	2	4	48	29	4	4	13	22	43	44	10th
1929/30	1	42	13	4	4	52	32	2	3	16	19	60	37	19th
1930/31	1	42	9	2	10	41	45	6	4	11	37	42	36	17th
1931/32	1	42	13	5	3	52	31	5	1	15	28	56	42	11th
1932/33	1	42	15	2	4	44	24	7	3	11	27	39	49	5th
1933/34	1	42	6	11	4	42	29	4	3	14	26	48	34	21st (Relegated)
1934/35	2	42	14	2	5	55	25	8	2	11	34	43	48	6th
1935/36	2	42	13	5	3	56	27	7	1	13	32	52	46	8th
1936/37	2	42	11	3	7	45	23	11	2	8	35	33	49	4th
1937/38	2	42	12	4	5	38	18	2	4	15	13	40	36	19th
1938/39	2	42	13	3	5	44	21	5	7	9	17	27	46	9th
1939/46						SECOND WORLD WAR								
1946/47	2	42	11	4	6	60	32	8	6	7	35	30	48	5th
1947/48	2	42	18	1	2	46	13	6	7	8	26	28	56	2nd (Promoted)
1948/49	1	42	12	5	4	35	29	8	7	6	35	27	52	4th
1949/50	1	42	14	4	3	49	23	5	8	8	28	32	50	5th
1950/51	1	42	10	6	5	36	22	8	7	6	26	31	49	4th
1951/52	1	42	12	4	5	62	28	6	5	10	36	45	45	8th
1952/53	1	42	9	5	7	34	33	5	4	12	25	37	37	16th
1953/54	1	42	9	2	10	43	40	5	8	8	29	37	38	15th
1954/55	1	42	12	5	4	53	27	5	4	12	36	50	43	8th
1955/56	1	42	12	4	5	49	24	5	3	13	36	46	41	11th
1956/57	1	42	10	5	6	43	31	4	3	14	24	56	36	17th
1957/58	1	42	6	4	11	38	42	6	4	11	35	39	32	19th
1958/59	1	42	11	3	7	40	29	6	4	11	40	51	41	11th
1959/60	1	42	10	5	6	42	32	8	3	10	40	46	44	8th
1960/61	1	42	7	7	7	51	49	4	3	14	35	60	32	21st (Relegated)
1961/62	2	42	10	5	6	40	27	5	4	12	24	31	39	11th
1962/63	2	42	11	8	2	48	23	7	3	11	31	36	47	7th
1963/64	2	42	14	2	5	49	26	6	3	12	25	43	45	8th
1964/65	2	42	16	4	1	50	16	8	5	8	31	29	57	1st (Promoted)
1965/66	1	42	10	5	6	26	20	4	4	13	24	43	37	15th
1966/67	1	42	9	5	7	24	27	3	4	14	15	54	33	20th
1967/68	1	42	12	7	2	38	20	1	8	12	16	47	41	10th
1968/69	1	42	12	7	2	40	20	3	7	11	21	35	44	9th
1969/70	1	42	14	2	5	42	16	3	11	7	15	19	47	7th
1970/71	1	42	9	9	3	27	16	5	4	12	17	30	41	12th
1971/72	1	42	10	6	5	30	18	5	5	11	19	34	41	11th

1972/73	1	42	12	6	3	35	19	4	7	10	25	32	45	9th
1973/74	1	42	9	6	6	28	21	4	6	11	21	27	38	15th
1974/75	1	42	12	4	5	39	23	3	5	13	20	49	39	15th
1975/76	1	42	11	4	6	51	26	4	5	12	20	36	39	15th
1976/77	1	42	14	6	1	40	15	4	7	10	24	34	49	5th
1977/78	1	42	4	6	11	26	37	2	4	15	16	41	22	21st
														(Relegated)
1978/79	2	42	13	3	5	35	24	4	5	12	16	31	42	8th
1979/80	2	42	13	6	2	35	19	2	8	11	18	30	44	9th
1980/81	2	42	11	7	3	22	13	3	7	11	8	32	42	11th
1981/82	2	42	14	4	3	30	14	4	4	13	22	36	62	9th
1982/83	2	42	13	6	2	43	21	5	7	9	32	32	67	5th
1983/84	2	42	16	2	3	51	18	8	6	7	34	35	80	3rd
														(Promoted)
1984/85	1	42	11	4	6	33	26	2	9	10	22	44	52	14th
1985/86	1	42	12	5	4	46	31	5	7	9	21	41	63	11th
1986/87	1	42	10	4	07	33	29	2	7	12	14	36	47	17th
1987/88	1	40	9	6	5	32	23	5	8	7	23	30	56	8th
1988/89	1	38	3	6	10	19	28	4	4	11	13	35	31	20th
														(Relegated)
1989/90	2	46	17	4	2	51	26	5	10	8	29	29	80	3rd
1990/91	2	46	8	10	5	24	22	6	7	10	25	34	59	11th
1991/92	2	46	9	8	6	38	30	4	5	14	28	54	52	20th
1992/93	(1)	46	16	6	1	58	15	13	3	7	34	23	96	1st
														(Promoted)
1993/94	Pr	42	14	4	3	51	14	9	4	8	31	27	77	3rd
1994/95	Pr	42	14	6	1	46	20	6	6	9	21	27	72	6th
1995/96	Pr	38	17	1	1	38	9	7	5	7	28	28	78	2nd
1996/97	Pr	38	13	3	3	54	20	6	8	5	19	20	68	2nd
1997/98	Pr	38	8	5	6	22	20	3	6	10	13	24	44	13th
1998/99	Pr	38	7	6	6	26	25	4	7	8	22	29	46	13th
1999/00	Pr	38	10	5	4	42	20	4	5	10	21	34	52	11th
2000/01	Pr	38	10	4	5	26	17	4	5	10	18	33	51	11th
2001/02	Pr	38	12	3	4	40	23	9	5	5	34	29	71	4th
2002/03	Pr	38	15	2	2	36	17	6	4	9	27	31	69	3rd
2003/04	Pr	38	11	5	3	33	14	2	12	5	19	26	56	5th
2004/05	Pr	38	7	7	5	25	25	3	7	9	22	32	44	14th
2005/06	Pr	38	11	5	3	28	15	6	2	11	19	27	58	7th
2006/07	Pr	38	7	7	5	23	20	4	3	12	15	27	43	13th